L. Wackett

Exploring Careers
Instructor's Guide

An Instructor's Guide to the Exploring Careers Series

- Self-assessment activities
- Skills identification
- Career interests based on school and other activities
- Career planning
- Training and education options
- Help in exploring over 300 jobs in 14 major clusters
- Sources of additional information

Designed for use with *Exploring Careers*, a comprehensive career reference book.

©1990, JIST Works, Inc., Indianapolis, Indiana. All rights reserved. No part of this book can be duplicated in any form without the express, written permission of the publisher.

How To Use This Book

Exploring Careers was written to assist young people in understanding themselves and what they want as they explore career alternatives. This instructor's guide, *Exploring Careers* reference guide, and its consumable student workbook are all easy to use and can be used either independently or as part of a career exploration class or program.

Ordering Information

Contact the publisher for details on current pricing and quantity discounts of the books in the *Exploring Careers* series:

1. *Exploring Careers—The World of Work and You* (consumable book)
2. *Exploring Careers* (reference book containing information on over 300 careers)
3. *Exploring Careers—Instructor's Guide*
4. *The Occupational Outlook Handbook* (revised every two years)

Qualified institutions can also request to obtain our free catalog of carefully evaluated career and job search materials from over 40 publishers including books, videos, software and instructional aids.

Use the order form that follows the table of contents or call us toll free at **1-800-648-JIST** (**1-317-637-6643** in Indiana, Canada and outside the continent al United States) during regular business hours, central time.

Exploring Careers—Instructor's Guide is based on content originally developed by the U.S. Department of Labor, Bulletin 2001.

720 North Park Avenue
Indianapolis, Indiana 46202-3431

This book has been revised by the editors of JIST Works, Inc.
REVISION CREDITS:
  Project Coordinator: J. Michael Farr
  Project Supervisor: Spring Dawn Reader
  Revision editors: JoAnn Amore, Gregg Croy, Lisa Farr
  Photography: Spring Dawn Reader

ISBN # 0-942784-28-4

To The Teacher:

The enclosed Activity Sheets and Exploration Activities pages have been created to complement the reference material in *Exploring Careers* (©1990, by JIST Works, Inc., Indianapolis, Indiana). These sheets may be copied in reasonable quantities for classroom use when used in conjunction with *Exploring Careers*. An answer key for the activities sheets has also been included in the final section.

The activity sheets may be used in several ways, depending on your implementation of the material. The following suggestions may be useful:

1. Distribute "Exploration Activity" sheets after the corresponding occupations or clusters are studied in *Exploring Careers*. Encourage students to follow some of the suggestions to explore occupations that interest them.

2. Copy a small quantity of each "Exploration Activity" and place in a magazine rack in your career center, library, or media center. Allow students to take sheets for occupations that interest them as they complete various exploration options individually. (You may want to use a different color paper for each of the 14 clusters.)

3. Use the "Exploration Activities" as ideas for class assignments, discussions, or quizzes.

4. Distribute the appropriate activity sheet as each occupation is studied.

5. Use the activity sheets as homework assignments or quizzes.

6. Make quantities of each activity sheet available for students to complete as they work through independent study projects.

A student guide explaining the importance of career exploration, which includes self awareness and self exploration activities, is also available from JIST Works, Inc. to complement these materials.

Table of Contents

Assembler 1
Machinist 3
Photocompositor 6
Bank Officer 9
Planner 12
Computer Programmer/Systems
　Analyst 14
Chef 16
Building Service Worker 20
Hotel Clerk 22
Police Officer 24
Librarian 26
Secondary School Teacher 28
School Counselor 31
Security Sales Worker 33
Parts Counter Worker 36
Gasoline Service Station Attendant . 38
Bricklayer 41
Carpenter 44
Plumber 47
Air Traffic Controller 50
Railroad Conductor 52
Bus Driver 54
Biochemist 56
Electrical Engineer 58
Broadcast Technician 60
Auto Mechanic 61
Computer Service Technician 63
Jeweler 65
Registered Nurse 67
Medical Technologist 71
Physical Therapist 74
Museum Curator 77
Political Aide 81
Minister 82
Social Worker 84
Architect 87
Newspaper Reporter 91
Musician 96
Farmer 99
Cooperative Extension Service
　Worker 103
Forester 106
Answer Key 108

ORDERING INSTRUCTIONS

- **CE3** *Exploring Careers* • Revised Edition • 500 pp. • **$19.95**
- **CE3G** *Exploring Careers — Instructor's Guide* • 117 pp. • **$12.95**
- **CE3S** *Exploring Careers — The World of Work and You* • 34 pp. • **$39.00**/pkg of 20

Other Career Reference Books Available:

- **OOH88H** *Occupational Outlook Handbook* • 456 pp. • Hardcover **$20.95**
- **OOH88** *Occupational Outlook Handbook* • 456 pp. • Softcover **$17.76**
- **CE17** *Guide For Occupational Exploration* — Second Edition • 984 pp. • **$26.50**
- **CE1** *Dictionary of Occupational Titles* • 1,371 pp. • **$31.00**
- **CE16** *4th Edition DOT Supplement* • 103 pp. • **$6.50**

Job Search Text/Workbooks Available:

- **RW** *Getting The Job You Really Want* • 138 pp. • **$7.95**
- **RWIG** *Getting The Job You Really Want — Instructor's Guide* • 64 pp. • **$12.95**
- **QJS** *The Quick Job Search* • 32 pp. • **$53.00**/pkg of 20

CODE TOTAL	QTY	TITLE	UNIT PRICE	

SHIPPING & HANDLING
Prepaid Orders Shipped Free!
Orders under $100 @ 15%
Orders between $100 & $499 @ 7.5%
Orders over $500 @ 5%

SUBTOTAL	
IN Residents add 5% Sales Tax	
SHIP & HANDLING	

jist: the job search people

Ship To:
Name _____ Title _____
Organization _____
Street Address* _____
City/State/Zip _____ Phone ( ) _____

*Orders cannot be delivered to P.O. Box via U.P.S.

Mail To: JIST Works, Inc. • 720 North Park Avenue • Indianapolis, Indiana 46202-3431

Phone Orders And Information: **1-800-648-JIST** or use **(317)637-6643** for calls from Indiana, Canada and outside the continental United States. Distributors, libraries, institutions, bookstores and individuals order from your dealer or from JIST Works, Inc. using the order form above. *Call for quantity discounts.* Orders from individuals must have $25 minimum. Prices are subject to change without notice. Orders must be prepaid unless previous credit arrangements have been made. MasterCard, VISA, American Express welcome. Call or send card #, expiration date, and name on the card with order.
***FAX* 1-317-264-3709.**

ASSEMBLER

A. Ask your teacher to arrange a plant tour if there is a factory in your community. Prepare questions in advance on the types of production jobs there. Ask about the education and training needed to get a job, starting pay, and opportunities for advancement.

B. Prepare a report on Henry Ford and the assembly line for your English or social studies class. Explain how this method of organizing work has affected the manufacturing process. How has it affected the workers?

C. Use *Working* by Studs Terkel as the subject for a book report in your English class. (New York: Pantheon Books, 1974.)

D. Prepare a report on industrial robotics for your English, social studies, or industrial arts class. Explain how this technology has affected the manufacturing process. How has the use of robots affected employment opportunities and worker requirements?

ASSEMBLER

ACTIVITY 1

Name _____
Class _____

ASSEMBLER
Related Occupations

Assemblers aren't the only workers with factory jobs. Using the descriptions below, unscramble the letters to find the names of other production workers. Write your answers on the lines provided.

1. **GIEWSN NAEMCIH TOAPRORE.** I use a sewing machine, to join, gather, hem, reinforce, or decorate such articles, as carpets, gloves, hats, bags, and upholstery.

   _____

2. **YAPSR NEITRAP.** I use a spray gun to spray the surfaces of machines, manufactured products, or working areas with paint, enamel, glaze, gelcoat, or lacquer. Before painting something, I often clean grease and dirt from it; sometimes I fill cavities and dents with putty.

   _____

3. **HAMNICE TURTEC.** I cut fabric into parts for such articles as canvas goods, house furnishings, garments, hats, stuffed toys, and upholstered furniture, using a portable electric cutter. I generally cut many layers of fabric at a time.

   _____

4. **CITAAMOUT NIRTP EPELOVERD.** I tend several machines that automatically develop, fix, wash, and dry photographic prints.

   _____

5. **CIAMNEH GAPARECK.** I tend machines that perform packaging functions, such as filling, marking, labeling, tying, packing, or wrapping containers.

   _____

6. **NARY DWENRI.** I tend machines that wind strands of yarn into packages for further processing, shipment, or storage.

   _____

7. **PLUMAOE RELFLI.** I tend a machine that fills small glass containers known as ampoules with measured doses of liquid drug products.

   _____

8. **ARCYN KEWROR.** I put fruits, vegetables, meat, cheese, and other food products into processing equipment—washing, peeling, refrigerating, coring, pitting, trimming, grinding, dicing, cooking, or slicing machines. The work I do is used in canning, freezing, preserving, or packaging food products.

   _____

9. **GTNTKINI HICANEM TROPAEOR.** I tend several machines that knit fabrics, garment parts, or other articles from yarn.

   _____

MACHINIST

A. Spend time on hobbies and other activities in which you build or repair things. Build models. Do carpentry. Sculpt. Make metal jewelry. Make repairs around your home. Repair your bicycle.

B. Volunteer to repair toys for a nursery school or day care center, or for a community organization such as the Salvation Army.

C. Join a chapter of VICA (Vocational Industrial Clubs of America), if your school has one. VICA chapters plan projects, take field trips, and hold competitions in such skill areas as machine shop and machine drafting.

D. Join an Auto Mechanic or Skilled Trades Explorer Post, if there is one in your area. Exploring is open to young men and women aged 14 through 20. To find out about Explorer posts in your area, call "Boy Scouts of America" listed in your phone book, and ask for the "Exploring Division."

E. If your school has a machine shop, ask the instructor to talk to your class. Arrange a tour of the shop.

F. If you are a Girl Scout, see if your local troop has the From Dreams to Reality program of career exploration. Troops may also offer opportunities to try out careers through internships, service aide and community action projects, and proficiency badges in a number of areas including Handywoman and Metal Arts.

G. If you are a Boy Scout, try for merit badges in Machinery, Metallurgy, Metalwork, and Model Design and Building.

H. Investigate the properties of metal for a report for your science class or for a science fair project. Compare the characteristics of several metals. Gold, for example, is relatively soft and easy to shape. Steel is harder and more difficult to work with. The encyclopedia is a good place to start your research. Public and school libraries have books that explain how different metals are made and used.

I. As a topic for a science or industrial arts class, report on machine tools such as lathes, milling machines, and drill presses. Illustrate your report with pictures and diagrams. The encyclopedia is a good place to get an overview of the topic. Library books will explain in more detail how machine tools work and what they are used for. Write for information to the National Machine Tool Builders Association, 7901 Westpark Drive, McLean, Virginia 22102.

J. Many foreign countries use the metric system of measurement. Therefore, some machinists must work in metrics to make parts which are compatible with imported products, or which will be suitable for export. Use the topic of metric measurement in metalworking for a report in a mathematics class. You might begin your research by writing for information to the Office of Weights and Measures, National Bureau of Standards, Washington, D.C. 20234. They also will supply a list, by State, of speakers to talk about the metric system.

Exploring Careers—Instructor's Guide ©1990, JIST Works, Inc., Indianapolis, Indiana

MACHINIST

ACTIVITY 2

Name _____
Class _____

MACHINIST
Related Occupations

Machinists are not only the workers who deal with metal and machines. Eight occupations in which the work is similar to a machinist's are listed below. Try to match the workers with their job titles. Write the letter of the correct answer on the lines provided.

    Machine tool operator   Mechanical engineer
    Instrument maker   Industrial machinery repairer
    Setup worker   Jeweler
    Tool-and-die maker   Watch repairer

1. Dan makes machines that are used for measurement in industrial production and research. He has all the skills of a machinist and more.
   _____

2. Brenda sets the speed on drill presses used by less skilled workers.
   _____

3. George works with precious metals. He can shape gold, silver, platinum just as a machinist shapes steel or brass.
   _____

4. Jim makes or repairs parts for a machine used by almost everyone. He uses a lathe just as a machinist does. The parts in his machine are so small that Jim uses a magnifying glass and tweezers to work with them.
   _____

5. Sarah designs machinery. She had to attend college to get her job.
   _____

6. Beverly makes the cutting devices used in machine tools. She learned many of her skills as a machinist.
   _____

7. Doug operates a drill press and grinding machine. He learned his skills on the job in a few months.
   _____

8. Susan repairs and maintains machines used in factories. Sometimes she uses machine tools to make replacement parts. Usually, however, she has the factory's machinist do the work.
   _____

©1990, JIST Works, Inc., Indianapolis, Indiana   *Exploring Careers—Instructor's Guide*

MACHINIST

ACTIVITY 3

Name _____
Class _____

MACHINIST
Math

Mathematics is an essential tool for machinists because precision is so important in their work. Machinists may work within tolerances as fine as 1/1,000 of an inch. To achieve this sort of precision, they make measurements and do calculations. See if you can solve the problems below. They are typical of some of the simpler problems machinists deal with every day. Write your answers on the lines provided.

1. A machinist must cut the following lengths from 2-meter bars of steel: 156 centimeters, 176 centimeters, 19 centimeters, 42 centimeters, and 117 centimeters. How many 2-meter bars will that take? How much steel will be left over?

   _____

2. In cutting gears for a piece of machinery, the number of teeth on a gear depends on the diameter of the wheel. A machinist has just made a gear with 50 teeth and a diameter of 10 inches. How many teeth would be on a gear with a diameter of 7 inches?

   _____

3. A machinist has been assigned to cut a groove in a metal block so that the depth beneath the groove is 2.5983 inches. The block is 2.7482 inches thick. After finishing the job, the machinist measures the groove and finds it is .1498 inches deep. In order to work, the part must have been machined to within a tolerance of 1/10,000 of an inch. Is the part acceptable?

   _____

Exploring Careers—Instructor's Guide   ©1990, JIST Works, Inc., Indianapolis, Indiana

PHOTOCOMPOSITOR

A. Ask your teacher to arrange a field trip to view the printing process at a local printing plant or newspaper.

B. Invite a compositor to speak to your class about his or her job. Ask the speaker to bring in galley proofs and explain the proofreader's marks.

C. Try your hand at printing, using one of the inexpensive printing kits you can obtain at hobby shops or department stores.
- Put your name or initials on greeting cards or stationery.
- Make business cards for the staff of your school newspaper or yearbook.
- Print letterhead stationery for a school club.
- Print publicity for a school event such as a career day, concert, science fair, or awards ceremony.
- Volunteer to print flyers, bulletins, and news releases for your church or temple, or for a community organization.

D. Use the silk-screen process to print a poster, greeting card, or gift enclosure. Design and print holiday wrapping paper.

E. Set up a printing business as a class project under the Junior Achievement (JA) program. This program gives high school students a chance to operate an actual business. JA printing companies typically do job printing or publish local newspapers or magazines. For more information, write to Junior Achievement, Inc., 45 Clubhouse Dr., Colorado Springs, CO 80906.

F. Your school system, or a nearby community college or technical institute, may offer courses in printing or graphic arts. If so, invite one of the instructors to speak to your class. Prepare questions in advance on the kinds of printing jobs there are in your community, and the training they require.

G. Join a chapter of VICA (Vocational Industrial Clubs of America), if your school has one. VICA chapters plan projects, take field trips, and hold competitions in such skill areas as offset printing.

H. Invite a local representative from the International Typographical Union to speak to your class about apprenticeship opportunities in the printing industry in your community.

I. If you are a boy scout, try for the merit badge in printing.

J. Computers and electronics are changing printing methods. Hobbies in these areas provide a good background for a career in the printing industry.
- Do a project on electronics or computers for a science fair.
- Join an Electronics or Computer Explorer Post, if there is one in your area. Exploring is open to young men and women aged 14 through 20. To find out about Explorer posts in your area, call "Boy Scouts of America" listed in your phone book, and ask for the "Exploring Division."

K. Knowledge of photography is increasingly important in the printing industry.
- Learn how to take pictures with a 35-mm camera.
- Join a Photography Explorer Post, if there is one in your area.
- If you are a Boy Scout, try for a merit badge in Photography.
- If you are a Girl Scout, see if your local troop has the From Dreams to Reality program of career exploration. Troops also offer proficiency badges in a number of areas, including photography.

PHOTOCOMPOSITOR

L. Artistic ability is necessary for the compositor in a small shop who does layout work. Design a collage or poster for a school activity or a community event.

M. As a project for an English or art class, set up a display of different types of printed material: Books, magazines, newspapers, flyers, matchbook covers, labels on containers and packages. For each item in your display, identify the type size and typeface. The library has books on typography that will help.

N. Use the topic of metrics in the graphic arts and printing trades for a report in a mathematics class. You might begin your research by writing for information to the Office of Weights and Measures, National Bureau of Standards, Washington, D.C. 20234. They also will supply a list, by state, of speakers to talk about the metric system.

O. As a project for an English or social studies class, report on the role of newspapers and the printing industry during the American Revolution.

P. Write for information on careers in the printing industry to the American Newspaper Publishers Association, The Newspaper Center, Post Office Box 17407, Dulles International Airport, Washington, D.C. 20041 and to the Graphic Arts Technical Foundation, Education Council of the Graphic Arts, 4615 Forbes Avenue, Pittsburgh, Pennsylvania 15213.

Exploring Careers—Instructor's Guide   ©1990, JIST Works, Inc., Indianapolis, Indiana

PHOTOCOMPOSITOR

ACTIVITY 4

Name _____
Class _____

PHOTOCOMPOSITOR
Related Occupations

The compositor handles only one step of a printing job. The work of other people in printing and publishing occupations is described below. Refer to the list of job titles below and write the correct title on the lines provided.

    Bookbinder   Layout artist
    Production manager   Photoengraver
    Printing press operator   Printing sales representative
    Proofreader

1. I run the printing press, inserting print plates into the machine and controlling the ink and paper. I also may have to clean or repair the machine. Who am I?

   _____

2. I check the type for all kinds of errors, such as spelling, grammar, punctuation, and margins. Who am I?

   _____

3. I make metal printing plates of pictures and other copy that cannot be set in type. Who am I?

   _____

4. I operate machinery that folds, sews, staples, and binds printed items. Who am I?

   _____

5. I deal with the public, trying to get new business for the printing company. Selling this service requires a knowledge of printing technology and the ability to advise customers about their particular needs. Who am I?

   _____

6. I take the manuscript and rough ideas from the client and then plan the design of the job. I prepare the job for the composing room workers. Who am I?

   _____

7. I oversee the entire production process, following each job from the planning stage to the delivery to the customer. I must see that we stick to the budget and time schedule set up for every job we do. Who am I?

   _____

BANK OFFICER

A. Arrange a class tour of a large bank. Talk to employees in several different departments. Find out how they started in banking, what they do, and how they fit into the total operation. Make a list of the different kinds of officers in the bank.

B. Invite officers from two or three departments of a bank to visit your class and present a panel discussion. Ask them to describe the work they do and the training they needed to get their jobs. Prepare questions for the panelists.

C. Serve as treasurer of a club or other organization. Volunteer to help collect and count money for a school event. This will give you experience handling money. By keeping a careful record of all the money received and spent, you can also learn something of bookkeeping.

D. Role-play a meeting between a loan officer and customer requesting an auto loan. Plan the roles ahead of time: How much money is requested and for how long? What is the borrower's financial situation? What questions does the loan officer ask? Use a loan application from your local bank.

E. As a topic for a report in your English, social studies, or mathematics class, investigate the difference between a bank and a savings and loan association. You might start by talking to an official of each. In your report, try to answer these questions: What do banks have in common with savings and loan associations? What services does each offer that the other does not? What laws apply to each? What occupations are found in one, but not the other?

F. When people think of money, they usually think of cash—coins and bills. In fact, most of the "money" in circulation in the United States is not in the form of cash, but in the form of approximately 25 billion checks written each year. Use checking as a topic for a report in your English, social studies, or mathematics class. Talk to your parents, your school or public librarian, and the officers of a local bank to find answers to these questions: How do you use a checking account? What happens to the check after it is written? (Make a diagram to illustrate this.) What happens if a check "bounces?" What kind of bank occupations are connected with checking accounts? Report the results of your investigation to your class.

G. What does "interest" mean to a banker? In the story you read, Bill explained to Mr. and Mrs. Lupovich that interest is the cost of borrowing money from the bank. But if they had a savings account, the bank would pay them interest for keeping their money there. Interest, quite simply, is the price someone (a person or bank) pays for using another's money.

H. Use the topic of interest and interest rates for a report to your English, social studies, or mathematics class. Answer the following questions: What interest rates do banks in your area set for loans? Why do they charge different rates for different kinds of loans? What interest rates do they set on different kinds of savings accounts? How do banks' rates compare with those of savings and loan associations?

I. Interview one of the officers at your local bank to find out how a 24-hour teller works. Ask whether the bank needed fewer people to work as tellers after the machine was installed. Report to the class, bringing with you examples of the different kinds of forms needed to conduct transactions with an automatic teller.

J. Have you ever looked closely at a dollar bill? Notice the words above George Washington's picture: Federal Reserve Note. They refer to the Federal Reserve System, or "Feds," which regulates the amount of money in circulation in the United States. Use the history of money as a topic for an individual or group report in your English, social studies, or mathematics class. Answer the following questions: When and how did your national currency come to be? How has it changed over the years? What gives paper and coin money its value? When and why was the Federal Reserve System created? How is it run? Who is its current leader? How does it regulate the amount of money in use?

BANK OFFICER

K. Join a Banking or Finance Explorer Post if there is one in your area. Exploring is open to young men and women aged 14 through 20. To find out about Explorer posts in your area, call "Boy Scouts of America" listed in your phone book, and ask for the "Exploring Division."

L. Write for information on careers in banking to the Bank Personnel Division, American Bankers Association, 1120 Connecticut Avenue, N.W., Washington, D.C. 20036.

BANK OFFICER

ACTIVITY 5

Name _____

Class _____

BANK OFFICER
Related Occupations

Bank officers are one of many kinds of workers who do detailed financial work. Several others are listed below, along with possible descriptions of what they do. For each occupation, see if you can choose the correct description. Circle the corresponding letter.

1. **Accountant**
   a. Prepares financial reports and tax returns for businesses or individuals.
   b. Opens new checking and savings accounts for customers at a bank.
   c. Counts freshly printed dollar bills at the U.S. Bureau of Engraving and Printing to be sure how many were made.

2. **Appraiser**
   a. Gives final approval to all requests by businesses for bank loans.
   b. Keeps track of bank employee's work and tells them when they are doing a good job.
   c. Determines the value of land and buildings for tax purposes.

3. **Auditor**
   a. Listens to the explanations of people who can't pay their bills on time.
   b. Inspects a company's records and reports on its financial situation.
   c. Tracks down people who write phony checks.

4. **Broker**
   a. Gives advice to people who have run out of money.
   b. Sells automobile insurance.
   c. Buys and sells stocks for people and businesses.

5. **Credit analyst**
   a. Checks up on newly hired bank tellers to make sure they can be trusted.
   b. Looks at the financial situations of people and businesses to see if they should receive credit.
   c. Helps people decide what credit cards to get.

6. **Revenue agent**
   a. Helps protect the gold at Fort Knox.
   b. Investigates cases of counterfeiting (printing phony money) for the FBI.
   c. Checks up on tax returns to make sure people and businesses are paying their taxes.

7. **Treasurer**
   a. Keeps track of how much cash a bank has each hour of the day.
   b. Directs the use of a company's money.
   c. Tells the President how much money is in the U.S. Treasury.

8. **Underwriter**
   a. Approves or denies a person's request for life insurance.
   b. Keeps a company's checkbook and signs all its checks.
   c. Helps a company find the best way to make money.

Exploring Careers—Instructor's Guide ©1990, JIST Works, Inc., Indianapolis, Indiana

PLANNER

A. As a project for your social studies or government class, find out if your city or town has a planning department. (If not, your county or a nearby town might). Invite one of the planners to speak to your class. Prepare questions beforehand about the process of planning and the work of planners. Be sure to find out what other parts of your local government are involved in the planning process.

B. As a topic for a report in your history, social studies, or government class, investigate the history of the area in which you live. Try to answer the following questions with your research: When was your city or town founded? Was there a special reason for its location? How did it grow to its present form? If your community is now planned, when and why did planning begin? The library and the local government should be able to help you find the information you need.

C. Use zoning as a topic for a report in your social studies or government class. You might go to a hearing before the local zoning authority as part of your research. In your report, try to answer these questions: How many different kinds of zones exist? What are some of them? What restrictions does the community set on height and spacing of buildings? Who makes zoning decisions? How can zones be changed? What role can the public play in making zoning decisions?

D. Using what you've learned about zoning in the preceding exercise, role-play a situation in which a developer wants to build a shopping center on land zoned for single-family homes. Students should work out and play the roles of the developer, merchants who want to open stores in the shopping center, the zoning authority, neighborhood residents opposed to the project, planners, and any others who come to mind.

E. As a project for your social studies or art class, design a park or playground for a vacant lot or field in your neighborhood. Make a scale drawing of your design, showing where you would place lawn, trees, pavement, playing fields, equipment, and buildings.

F. Have a panel discussion in your social studies class on a new project proposed for your area, such as a new shopping center, a dam, or a recreational area. (If no suitable project exists, your teacher can suggest an imaginary one). The discussion should center on these questions: How will the project benefit the community? How will it hurt? Are the benefits worth the cost? What changes in the project would you suggest to make it more beneficial?

G. Put together a group report in your science or social studies class on air and water pollution in your community, dealing with these questions: How bad is the pollution? How is it measured? What are the proper sources? What is being done about it? Talk to people with different interests and points of view: Government officials; public relations representatives from power companies; local industry officials; and citizen groups concerned with environmental quality. The class can be divided into smaller groups to gather information.

H. Join a Government or Politics Explorer Post if there is one in your area. Exploring is open to young men and women aged 14 through 20. To find out about Explorer posts in your area, call "Boy Scouts of America" listed in your phone book, and ask for the "Exploring Division."

I. Write for information on careers in planning to the American Society of Planning Officials, 1313 East 60th Street, Chicago, Illinois 60637 and to the American Institute of Planners, 1776 Massachusetts Avenue, N.W., Washington, D.C. 20036.

PLANNER

ACTIVITY 6

Name _____
Class _____

PLANNER
Related Occupations

Planners aren't the only people with jobs that involve planning and design. Seven other occupations are listed below. See if you can match each item with the worker who would plan or design it. Write your answer in the space provided.

A golf course
A dam
A computer system to figure salaries and issue paychecks
An improved production method for a chocolate factory

A survey of the breakfast cereals people eat
The styling and upholstery of an automobile
A house

1. Architect
   _____

2. Civil engineer
   _____

3. Computer systems analyst
   _____

4. Industrial designer
   _____

5. Industrial engineer
   _____

6. Landscape architect
   _____

7. Market researcher
   _____

Exploring Careers—Instructor's Guide ©1990, JIST Works, Inc., Indianapolis, Indiana

COMPUTER PROGRAMMER/SYSTEMS ANALYST

A. Arrange for a programmer or analyst to come and speak to your mathematics or science class about his or her work. A major bank, industrial firm, or computer company is a good place to find such a person.

B. Present a report on computers to your mathematics or science class. Include a brief history of computers and an explanation of their main parts. A diagram would help your presentation. Also explain the differences between: Input and output; analog and digital computers; hardware and software.

C. Computers are an important tool in many different fields. Report to your mathematics, science, or social studies class on how they are used in one of these areas: Teaching, crime control, banking, medicine, transportation, or scientific research.

D. Can a computer think? Talk about different aspects of this question in a social studies or English class report or panel discussion. To prepare, consider these questions: What does it mean to "think?" How does a computer make decisions? How do people make decisions?

E. As a topic for a report in your math class, discuss the binary system of numbers. Be sure to explain how computers use the binary system and how it differs from the decimal system. Also include examples of binary addition.

F. As a topic for a report in your math class, find out what a flow chart is and how it is used. Draw a flow chart of a simple system, such as your system for getting ready for school in the morning, or a system for planning and cooking a meal.

G. Join a Computer Explorer Post, if there is one in your area. Exploring is open to young men and women aged 14 through 20. To find out about Explorer posts in your area, call "Boy Scouts of America" listed in your phone book, and ask for the "Exploring Division."

H. Write for information on careers in programming and systems analysis to the American Federation of Information Processing Societies, 1999 Preston White Dr., Reston, VA 22091 or the Association for Systems Management, 24587 Bagley Rd., Cleveland, OH 44138.

COMPUTER PROGRAMMER/SYSTEMS ANALYST

ACTIVITY 7

Name _____

Class _____

COMPUTER PROGRAMMER/SYSTEMS ANALYST
Related Occupations

Mathematics and statistics are very important in the work of computer programmers and systems analysts, but many other workers use math and statistics, too. Six of them describe their jobs below. See if you can figure out who they are. To help you, there is a list of the six occupations. Write your answer in the space provided.

Actuary
Financial analyst
Mathematical technician

Mathematician
Operations research analyst
Statistician

1. My job is doing basic research in mathematics. I develop new ideas and techniques in algebra, geometry, topology, and other branches of math. My discoveries are used widely in science, engineering, and many other fields. Who am I?

   _____

2. I work for an insurance company. I figure out how often different groups of drivers—young drivers, city drivers, truckdrivers, and sports car drivers, for example—have accidents. The company uses this information to set the prices of its insurance policies. Who am I?

   _____

3. When a business is not running smoothly, I use mathematics and computers to solve the problem. First I find out from the managers exactly what the trouble is. Then I make a mathematical model of the situation and feed it to the computer, which helps me find possible solutions. After comparing these I make my recommendations. Who am I?

   _____

4. I work for a company doing scientific research. The scientists collect large quantities of raw information from their experiments. With the help of computers and mathematical formulas, I reduce and convert this information into a more usable form. Who am I?

   _____

5. I help scientists gather reliable statistics for their research. I plan and conduct surveys to collect the information. Then I analyze the results to see how reliable they are. Computers help me a great deal. Who am I?

   _____

6. I work for a corporation that invests a great deal of money in the stock market. My job is to advise the company how best to spend its money. I study the market and my company's financial situation. I collect information, write reports, and make recommendations. Who am I?

   _____

Exploring Careers—Instructor's Guide ©1990, JIST Works, Inc., Indianapolis, Indiana

CHEF

A. Get the recipe for the same dish from two different cookbooks. Follow them both and compare the results. What differences do you notice in ingredients, methods of preparation, and the final dish?

B. Plan and prepare dinner for your family one night. You might want to pick a foreign country or a region of the United States and prepare all the food in this style. Notice how much planning ahead you have to do: Deciding on the menu, looking up recipes, and assembling the ingredients.

C. Experiment with cooking the same food in various ways and observe the differences. Vegetables, for example, can be boiled, steamed, baked, sauteed, or deep fried.

D. Learn what to look for in selecting meats, fish, poultry, fruits, and vegetables for quality and freshness.

E. Enter a baking or cooking contest.

F. Offer to help in a food co-op if there is one in your neighborhood. You can gain valuable experience in ordering food, picking up merchandise, and keeping inventory.

G. Volunteer to help in the school cafeteria.

H. Volunteer your services to your local Meals-on-Wheels program. Volunteers are needed to deliver meals to people's homes; they may also help with food preparation, packaging, and clerical work.

I. Invite one or more food service workers to speak to your class about their jobs. You might invite the manager of the school cafeteria; a chef or cook at a local restaurant; or the manager of a fast-food restaurant. Ask them to describe the work they do and the training they needed to get their jobs. Prepare questions in advance.

J. Contact your local health department and invite a health inspector to speak to your class. Inspectors visit restaurants regularly to check the cleanliness and safety of food served to the public. You might ask the speaker to discuss his or her job and the training needed to get the job; to explain what inspectors look for when they inspect a restaurant; and to tell you what would be sufficient cause to close a restaurant down. Prepare questions in advance.

K. Prepare a report on the sources of some familiar seasonings and spices for a social studies class. You might start your research by looking in the encyclopedia, then write for information to one of the companies that package and distribute herbs and spices.

L. For science or health class, prepare a report on the importance of vitamins, carbohydrates, fats, calories, and protein to your body. Explain the way in which each of these helps to maintain your metabolism. (Metabolism is the process by which your body breaks down the food you eat for its energy.)

M. Use the topic of bacteria growth in food for a science fair project.

N. Determine the nutritional value of a typical fast-food meal—a hamburger, milkshake, and French fries, for example. How does this compare with the recommended daily requirements?

O. Plan the layout and design of a printed menu.

P. Learn the four food groups and match the foods you eat during the day with their proper group.

Q. Make a list of safety and first aid rules that should be observed in the kitchen; for example, what to do in case of a fire and how to treat cuts and burns.

CHEF

R. Join a chapter of VICA (Vocational Industrial Clubs of America) if your school has one. VICA chapters plan projects, take field trips, and hold competitions in such skill areas as cooking.

S. Join a chapter of HERO (Home Economics Related Occupations) if your school has one. HERO chapters help students relate their home economics curriculum to careers. If your school does not have a chapter, you can ask your home economics teacher to sponsor one. Your teacher can obtain information by writing FHA/HERO Chapters, 2010 Massachusetts Avenue, N.W., Washington, D.C. 20036.

T. If you are a Boy Scout or Girl Scout, try for badges in Cooking and First Aid.

U. For information about a career as a chef, write to: Culinary Institute of America, P.O. Box 53, Hyde Park, New York 12538; Educational Director, Educational Foundation of the National Restaurant Association, 20 N. Wacker Dr., Chicago, Illinois 60606; or Educational Institute of the American Hotel and Motel Association, 1407 South Harrison Rd., East Lansing, Michigan 48823. For information on the American Culinary Federation's apprenticeship program for cooks and chefs, write to: American Culinary Federation, P.O. Box 3466, St. Augustine, FL 32084.

CHEF

ACTIVITY 8

Name _____
Class _____

CHEF
Related Occupations

Besides the chef, many other workers are involved in planning meals and preparing food. The following puzzle includes 18 of these occupations. See how many you can find. The words may be forwards or backwards, and horizontal, vertical, or diagonal. As you find each occupation circle it.

Baker	**Caterer**	**Roast Cook**	**Specialty Cook**
Banquet Chef	**Dessert Cook**	**Salad Maker**	**Soup Cook**
Barbecue Cook	**Executive Chef**	**Sauce Chef**	**Sous Chef**
Broiler Cook	**Fry Cook**	**Short Order Cook**	**Vegetable Cook**
Cafeteria Cook	**Pastry Chef**		

```
O K O C A F E T E R I A C O O K E H C
B R O I L E R C O O K P H I X Y F E P
A A P E S N V A O A S O L C R U Q F D
N R K X O T H P A S T R Y C H E F U E
Q B O E T E I K N T W Y H B E M R T S
U X C C R O H T A C R K E G I R Y Z S
E Z D U R N Y C F O O V O V E C C H E
T E L T E R B E R O C O L K Y F O I R
C M F I I T H B C K K X A B E R O N T
H G N V B C K P L E G M E H T U K J C
E O H E E A U G L N D R S O L P Q C O
F I P C B O W D Y A O O R J U Z R B O
S Q U H S L D E L I P D C H E Q U R K
R A V E G E T A B L E C O O K N M P Y
S D E F C I S H O R T C M P O S I T S
M L U C E S P E C I A L T Y C O O K P
A N O V A J K O O C E U C E B R A B I
S R Q U X S O U S C H E F P Y Q U L L
V T G H A K O C Y H L N C A T E R E R
```

©1990, JIST Works, Inc., Indianapolis, Indiana — *Exploring Careers—Instructor's Guide*

CHEF

ACTIVITY 9 Name _____
 Class _____

CHEF
Math

Assume that you are head chef in a restaurant. A cookbook gives the following recipe for stew to feed six people. Write your answers in the space provided.

2 lbs. stew meat	1 large onion
2 lbs. potatoes	1 teaspoon salt
5 large carrots	1 cup mixed vegetables

1. How much of each ingredient will you need to feed 60 people?

   _____

2. How much must you spend if food prices are $1.49 per pound for stew meat, $.35 per pound for potatoes, $.05 each for carrots, $.15 each for onions, $.01 per teaspoon of salt, and $.30 per cup of mixed vegetables?

   _____

3. Assume you can get a 25-percent discount because you buy in large quantities. How much will your food bill be to make stew for 60 people?

   _____

4. In restaurants, ingredients often are measured by weight instead of volume because this method is simpler and more accurate. Find the following measurements:

   a. 1 teaspoon butter = approximately

      _____ grams.

   b. 1 tablespoon salt = approximately

      _____ grams.

   c. 1 cup flour = approximately

      _____ grams.

BUILDING SERVICE WORKER

A. Help with minor plumbing repairs at home. Help replace a washer in a leaky faucet. Clean out a sink trap. Your public library has books on home repairs that can guide you.

B. Help family and friends with automobile engine repairs. Do your own repair work for your bicycle. Mechanical work of this kind will give you practice working with small handtools.

C. Ask your parents to teach you to operate household appliances properly—a vacuum cleaner, rug shampooer, floor buffer, or lawn mower, for example.

D. Help with the gardening at home. You can assist with fertilizing and mowing the lawn, trimming trees and bushes, planting flowers and vegetables, and weeding.

E. Organize a cleanup campaign and pick up litter around your schoolyard or in a nearby park. This could be a class or club project.

F. Volunteer to repair toys at a day care center, Headstart program, or nursery school.

G. Offer to do minor home repairs or help winterize the homes of elderly neighbors. There may be a program of this kind in your community to which you could donate your services. To find out, call the local voluntary action center or agency on aging.

H. Help renovate a room or building for a teen club or community center.

I. Set up a schedule of the chores you do around your home each week, allotting a certain amount of time for each one. See how close your estimates come to the time it actually takes.

J. Interview one of the building service workers at your school about his or her job. See if you can arrange to "shadow" him or her for a morning or afternoon. Report back to your class.

K. Invite a representative of a commercial cleaning firm to speak to your class about his or her business. Prepare questions in advance.

L. If you are a Girl Scout, try for the Handywoman proficiency badge.

M. If you are a Boy Scout, try for the Home Repair and Plumbing merit badges.

BUILDING SERVICE WORKER

ACTIVITY 10

Name _____
Class _____

BUILDING SERVICE WORKER
Related Occupations

Building service workers aren't the only people who take care of buildings and the grounds around them. Unscramble the letters below to find the names of 12 other workers whose jobs involve cleaning buildings and keeping them in good repair. Write your answers in the space provided.

1. REEPKUOHSEE
   _____

2. GRDAENRE
   _____

3. TPRIEVA HOOLDUSHE REKROW
   _____

4. LOBIRE TEDRNE
   _____

5. TNAERPI
   _____

6. SEPT COOTLRLNRE
   _____

7. NTAIEMNNCEA CTNICEAELRI
   _____

8. AHSTR LLECCOTOR
   _____

9. LOFOR WRAEX
   _____

10. NAIJTRO
    _____

11. BDINUILG SUNEDTENTPINER
    _____

12. WONDIW CLNEERA
    _____

Exploring Careers—Instructor's Guide   ©1990, JIST Works, Inc., Indianapolis, Indiana

HOTEL CLERK

A. If you live in or near a city with a large hotel, arrange a tour for your class. Ask to see the front desk and other operations, such as housekeeping, mail delivery, reservations, and food preparation. Ask questions about how the hotel is managed.

B. Invite a hotel clerk or manager to come to your school and talk to your class. Prepare questions in advance.

C. Try an activity or job in which you deal with the public. There are several to choose from. For example:
- Join a club at your school, church, or synagogue that does community service work.
- Volunteer to collect money door to door for a charity or other cause.
- Sell something door to door, such as seeds or candy.
- Get a newspaper route. (The public contact comes each month when you collect money for the newspaper.)
- Get a job selling tickets or ushering at a movie theater.

D. Role-play a situation in which a hotel room clerk faces several angry, upset guests. The "guests" should prepare their "complaints" beforehand. After playing the roles, discuss what happened. How well did the "clerk" handle the guests? Should he or she have done anything differently?

E. Write for information on careers in the hotel and motel industry to Educational Institute of the American Hotel and Motel Association, 1407 South Harrison Road, East Lansing, Michigan 48823.

HOTEL CLERK

ACTIVITY 11

Name _____
Class _____

HOTEL CLERK
Related Occupations

Many kinds of workers serve, help, or provide information to the public. Hotel room clerks are one. The names of 12 others are hidden in the array of letters below. See if you can find them. They may be forwards or backwards, horizontal or vertical. Shade or circle each answer.

Customer Complaint Clerk	Reservation Clerk
Customer Service Representative	Sightseeing Guide
Flight Attendant	Theater Usher
Information Clerk	Ticket Agent
Passenger Train Conductor	Tour Guide
Receptionist	Travel Agent

Exploring Careers—Instructor's Guide ©1990, JIST Works, Inc., Indianapolis, Indiana

POLICE OFFICER

A. Many communities have a "Ride-Along" program in which you ride with a police officer for an evening. Call your local police department and ask for the officer in charge of community relations to find out whether there is a "Ride-Along" program where you live. If not, an informal ride with an officer might be possible.

B. Ask your teacher to arrange a class tour of your local police department. If you are in Washington, D.C., visit the FBI.

C. Invite a police officer to talk to your class about his or her job. Ask the speaker to explain the training and personal qualifications needed to join the police force in your community. Prepare questions in advance.

D. Invite a lawyer to speak to your class about our system of criminal justice and the way it works. What is the role of the police? Lawyers? The courts? Prisons and reformatories?

E. What "constitutional rights" must people be informed of when they are arrested? Prepare a report on this subject for a social studies class. The school library is a good place to start. And get in touch with your local police department to see what information they can provide.

F. Go to court and watch a trial. Report to your social studies class on the things you observed. You might describe a lawyer examining a witness, a cross examination, a jury reporting its verdict, or a judge pronouncing a sentence.

G. Role-play a situation that a police officer might face—a motorist going too fast, for example, or a shopper suspected of shoplifting.

H. Volunteer at a halfway house or a juvenile home. You might help organize recreation and games, do tutoring, handle clerical duties, teach arts and crafts or music, or accompany a group on special trips. For more information on places in your community that need volunteers, contact your local voluntary action center.

I. Learn how to take fingerprints. Why is fingerprinting so important in police work?

J. Role-play a police artist drawing a criminal suspect from the description given by an eyewitness.

K. Join an Explorer Post in Law Enforcement, Emergency First Aid, Emergency Service, or Search and Rescue. Exploring is open to young men and women aged 14 through 20. To find out about Explorer posts in your area, call "Boy Scouts of America" listed in your phone book, and ask for the "Exploring Division."

L. If you are a Boy Scout, try for merit badges in Citizenship in the Community, Emergency Preparedness, Fingerprinting, First Aid, Law, Personal Fitness, Public Speaking, and Safety.

M. If you are a Girl Scout, see if your local troop has the From Dreams to Reality program of career exploration. Troops also may offer opportunities to try out careers through internships, service aide, and community action projects.

N. Write for information about a career as a police officer to the International Association of Chiefs of Police, 13 Firstfield Road, Gaithersburg, Maryland 20878.

POLICE OFFICER

ACTIVITY 12

Name _____
Class _____

POLICE OFFICER
Related Occupations

Patrolling a beat is only one of many types of jobs a police officer may have. The jobs of 10 other people concerned with law enforcement are hidden below. See if you can break the code and figure them out. Write your answers in the space provided. You can start by using this hint:

B = A   P = O
F = E   V = U
J = I   Z = Y

1. EFUFDUJWF. _____

2. QPMJDF QIPUPHSBQIFS. _____

3. GCJ TQFDJBM BHFOU. _____

4. TIFSJGG. _____

5. QSPCBUJPO PGGJDFS. _____

6. TUBUF QPMJDF USPPQFS. _____

7. QPMJDF DIJFG. _____

8. DPNNVOJUZ SFMBUJPOT PGGJDFS. _____

9. QPMJDF BDBEFNZ JOTUSVDUPS. _____

10. GJOHFSQSJOU TQFDJBMJTU. _____

Exploring Careers—Instructor's Guide   ©1990, JIST Works, Inc., Indianapolis, Indiana

LIBRARIAN

A. *Read.* Use your school and public libraries to familiarize yourself with as many different subjects and styles of writing as possible.

B. Volunteer to work in a library. Many schools and public libraries use volunteers to shelve books, work at the circulation desk, and take care of other clerical jobs. Volunteers also help with story hours, set up displays, and deliver books to people in hospitals and nursing homes.

C. Working with the public often is an important part of a librarian's job. To see whether this appeals to you take advantage of opportunities to work with children.
- Take baby-sitting jobs.
- Offer to help with younger children at a nursery school, day care center, or summer recreational program.
- Volunteer to tutor elementary school programs.

D. Invite a librarian to speak to your class about his or her work and training. You might invite a librarian or media specialist from your school, a librarian from your public library, or a special librarian. If possible, invite several speakers and arrange a panel discussion of the similarities and differences in librarian's jobs.

E. Chances are that you're already familiar with your school library and public library. To learn more about the different kinds of libraries there are, try to arrange a class tour of a special library in your community. This could be a law library, a medical library, a music library, a map library, the library of a historical society, a rare books library, or a technical library in a business firm or research organization.

F. Use school assignments to learn more about libraries.
- Find out what services your public library offers the handicapped, the elderly, and other groups in your community. Ask about outreach programs, talking books, large print collections, and foreign language collections, for example. Report your findings to an English or social studies class.
- Report on the origins of the public library system in the United States for an English or social studies assignment.
- Library automation could be a topic for a report in a mathematics, English, or social studies class. Find out how computers are used in libraries for ordering and processing library materials, cataloging them, keeping track of circulation records, and providing "instant" information in response to requests.

G. Girl Scout or Boy Scout badge programs offer a chance to learn more about such subjects as art, astronomy, child care, citizenship, electricity, languages, and writing. Being familiar with a variety of topics will help you develop the broad background that librarians need.

H. Role-play a meeting between a public library director and local government officials who provide the funds for the library system. Decide in advance whether the meeting is a small one, attended by only a few library and government officials, or whether it's a public meeting attended by a large number of concerned citizens. Following are examples of topics that might be discussed.
- The need for a bookmobile to provide services to people who cannot get to the library.
- Whether or not to include a particular book, on a controversial subject, in the library's collection.

LIBRARIAN

ACTIVITY 13

Name _____
Class _____

LIBRARIAN
Related Occupations

Is a library career for you? The work of eight librarians is described below. Try to match each description with the correct job title. Write your answers in the space provided.

Acquisitions librarian
Bibliographer
Bookmobile librarian
Chief librarian

Classifier
Media specialist
Medical librarian
Reference librarian

1. Alice organizes library resources in a junior high school. Besides books, she works with magazines, newspapers, charts, films, maps, records, and many other materials.

   _____

2. Bill helps researchers by preparing lists of books, magazine articles, unpublished reports, and other sources of information on a particular topic. He often includes a brief summary of the contents of each item on his list. Sometimes he uses the library's computer to get a listing of all the relevant material. Other times, he searches for titles in the card catalog.

   _____

3. George examines new library materials and classifies them according to subject matter. He decides which classification numbers and headings should go on the cards that will be put in the card catalog. Although the library where George works used the Dewey Decimal system, he's familiar with other methods of organizing library materials as well.

   _____

4. Ed reads book reviews, publishers' announcements, and catalogs and decides which publications to order for his library. He sometimes gets ideas for new purchases from other librarians or library users.

   _____

5. Karen is the person with all the answers. If she doesn't know the answer to a patron's question, she knows where to look.

   _____

6. Lou brings his library to his readers.

   _____

7. Nancy works in a university medical center. The people who use her library need a librarian who knows the technical "language" used in the health sciences field.

   _____

8. Sally is responsible for everything that happens in her branch library.

   _____

Exploring Careers—Instructor's Guide   ©1990, JIST Works, Inc., Indianapolis, Indiana

SECONDARY SCHOOL TEACHER

A. Get involved in activities that give you an opportunity to develop teaching and leadership skills. Volunteer to tutor your classmates or younger students in a subject that interests you. Volunteer to help with children at a Head Start program, day care center, or nursery. Offer to direct children in arts and crafts, music, or sports in a summer recreational program. Participate in extracurricular activities in which you work with other students, such as school clubs, the school paper, or the school yearbook.

B. Talk to several secondary school teachers about their jobs. Find out why they became teachers, how they feel about the subjects they teach, how they feel about the students, and what they like and dislike about teaching. Ask elementary school teachers the same questions and compare answers.

C. If you know the subject you would like to teach, talk to the teacher who teaches it in your school. Find out why he or she teaches that subject. Ask for a list of books you could read to learn more about the subject.

D. Use school assignments to learn more about teaching.
- Prepare a report on the growth of public education in the United States for a history class.
- Prepare a report on current issues in education for an English or social studies class.
- Prepare a report on the use of computers in education for a science class.

E. Join an Education or Teaching Explorer Post, if there is one in your area. Exploring is open to young men and women aged 14 through 20. To find out about Explorer posts in your area, call "Boy Scouts of America" listed in your phone book and ask for the "Explorer Division."

F. If you are a Girl Scout, see if your local troop has the From Dreams to Reality program of career exploration. Troops may also offer opportunities to try out careers through internships, service aide and community action projects, and proficiency badges.

G. Teachers deal with many people in many different situations. Role-play the following situations to get a better idea of the teacher's point of view.
- A teacher correcting a student who continually disrupts class.
- A teacher explaining to a student's parents why the student failed the course.
- A teacher discussing a new course with the school principal.

H. Write for career information to American Federation of Teachers. 555 New Jersey Ave., NW, Washington, D.C. 20001.

SECONDARY SCHOOL TEACHER

ACTIVITY 14

Name _____

Class _____

SECONDARY SCHOOL TEACHER
Related Occupations

How many kinds of teachers are there? You probably can name quite a few just from the teachers in your school—athletic coach, biology teacher, history teacher, typing teacher, and more. If you add the elementary school, college, and adult education teachers that you know about, the list becomes even longer. But your list still would include only some of the occupations in teaching. For every subject people want to learn, there is some type of teacher.

The scrambled letters below contain the names of fourteen teachers. Each teaches a subject that is important in one of the fourteen occupational clusters in Exploring Careers. First unscramble the letters to find the job title. Then match the job with the right occupational cluster. Write the answers to the word scramble on the first line and the Occupational Cluster on the second line.

Occupational Clusters

Agriculture, Forestry, and Fisheries	**Sales**
Construction	**Performing Arts, Design, and Communications**
Education	**Scientific and Technical**
Health	**Service**
Industrial Production	**Social Scientists**
Mechanics and Repairers	**Social Service**
Office	**Transportation**

1. TRIALDUSIN STAR ERTEAHC.

   _____

   _____

2. GNIOOCK ERTEAHC.

   _____

   _____

3. RARYLIB SECNCEI ERTEAHC.

   _____

   _____

4. WLA FESSORPOR.

   _____

   _____

5. DELMOING CHAETER.

   _____

   _____

6. NILGYF ROICSUNTRT.

   _____

   _____

SECONDARY SCHOOL TEACHER

7. GINGINEENER CHAETER.

8. HCTAWMAKNIG CHAETER.

9. SINGRUN AHCRETE.

10. ONOCEMICS AHCRETE.

11. MONOCEMIHCOS AHCRETE.

12. TAR ETEAHCR.

13. ROFTESYR ETEAHCR.

14. PHOS TMAH ETEAHCR.

SCHOOL COUNSELOR

A. Involve yourself in a program or organization that is concerned with social problems in your community: Illiteracy, juvenile delinquency, education and recreation for the handicapped, friendly visiting and escort service for the elderly. This will test your interest in helping others.

B. Volunteer to help with clerical tasks in a hot-line crisis center. If you can show yourself to be a particularly mature, responsible teen, you may be given an opportunity to take the training and become a telephone listener.

C. Volunteer to work in a half-way house.

D. Volunteer to help with recreation programs sponsored by the YMCA, YWCA, your local government, or neighborhood centers.

E. Get in touch with the American National Red Cross about opportunities to work as a youth volunteer. Red Cross youth volunteers serve as tutors for younger children and as aides in day care centers; help with community programs related to drug abuse among young people; and play and study with homebound and handicapped children.

F. Contact the Boys' Club or Girls' Club in your community. Clubs offer a wide variety of programs including work with retarded and handicapped children. Work with handicapped youngsters will help you build experience for future rehabilitation counseling.

G. Volunteer to work in your school counseling center during a free hour.

H. Ask your school counselor if you may observe a session in which he/she helps a student with college selection or occupational information. Think about your own goals for the future as you observe.

I. Using what you've learned about counseling in the preceding exercise, role-play a situation in which a student wants some information or prospective colleges or occupational choices. Plan the roles ahead of time. What questions does the counselor ask about interests? About skills? About training? What questions does the student ask about colleges? Occupations?

J. Invite the school counselor to speak to your class. Ask for a description of the work as well as training requirements. Prepare questions ahead of time.

K. Take part in a group activity designed to promote self-sufficiency and self-awareness. If you are a Girl Scout, find out if your troop has the From Dreams to Reality program, which promotes self-exploration through career awareness. If you are a Boy Scout, you may want to take part in the High Adventure program. Outward Bound retreats are also designed to encourage self-sufficiency.

L. Put yourself in the helper role on a daily basis. This may involve listening to a friend talk through a problem, visiting an invalid in the hospital, or becoming a Big Sister or Big Brother to a disadvantaged or handicapped child in your community.

M. Talk to your friends about their college or career ideas for the future. Take note of the different visions. Discuss the importance of planning for good occupational choices.

N. Read books and magazines on the counseling field. Test your interest.

O. Write for career information to the American School Counselors Association, 5999 Stevenson Ave., Alexandra, VA 22304.

SCHOOL COUNSELOR

ACTIVITY 15

Name _____
Class _____

SCHOOL COUNSELOR
Related Occupations

School counselors are not the only people whose jobs involve helping others. Combine the following pictures of objects, signs, letters, and so forth and discover the names of five other occupations. Write your answers in the space provided.

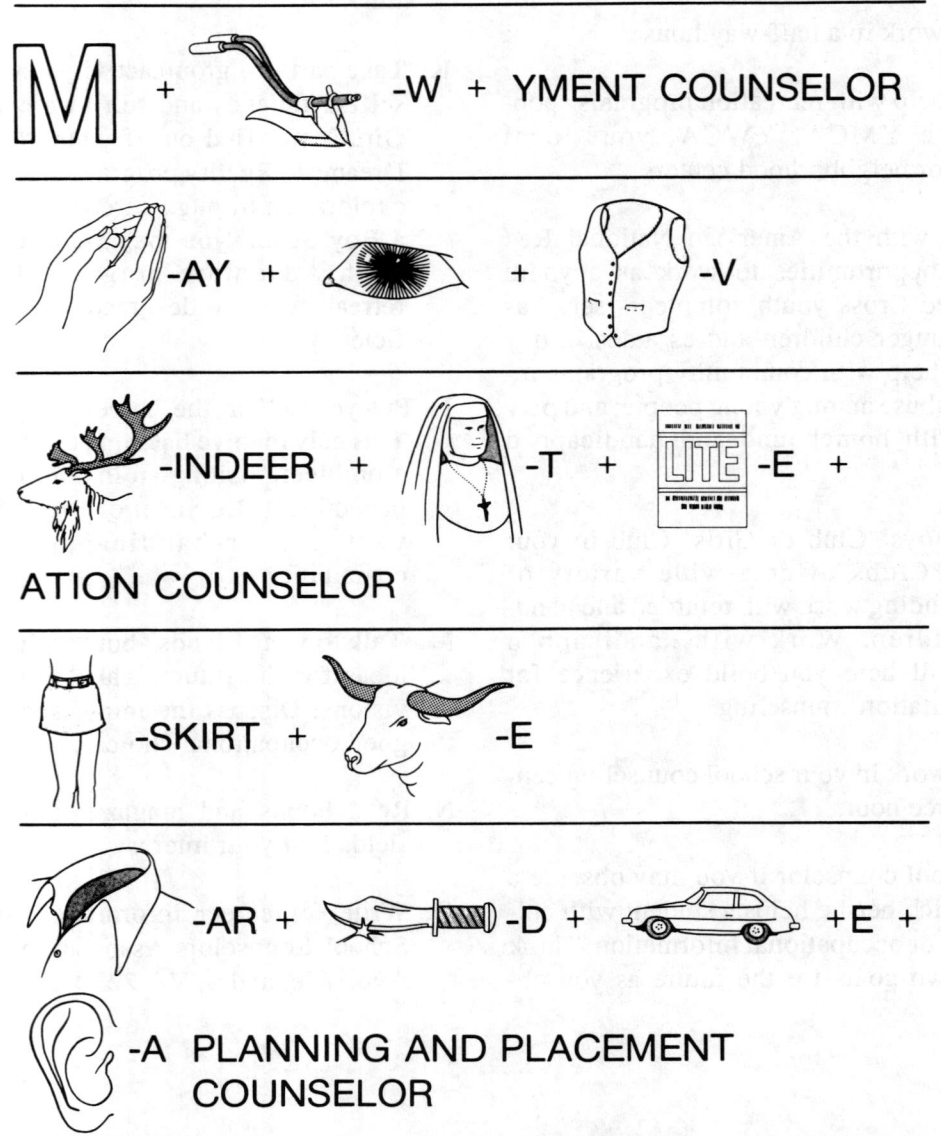

SECURITY SALES WORKER

A. Look in the financial section of your newspaper. Do the news stories in this section interest you? Can you understand the stock tables on the previous day's activities on the various exchanges?

B. Are there any large companies based in your home town? If so, try to find them in the stock tables.

C. Visit a brokerage office in your community. While you are there, observe the surroundings. What are the brokers doing? Are they on the phone a lot? How do they dress?

D. Go to your school or public library and look for books or pamphlets on investing in securities.

E. The price-earnings (P-E) ratio for a stock is determined by dividing a stock's price by the amount of money each share earned over the past year. For example, a stock selling at $25 that earned $5 would have a P-E of 5. Look up the P-E ratios for five different stocks in your newspaper's financial section. Do all stocks have the same P-E ratios? What could be some of the reasons for the differences?

F. Pretend that you have just been given $1,000 to invest. Select a stock or stocks that you like and determine how many shares you can buy. Chart the value of your stocks over a period of time. How did you choose your stocks? How much money did you make or lose?

G. The Dow Jones Industrial average is one measure of stock market performance. Go to your library and see if you can find a chart showing the Dow's performance over the past 25 years. Can you identify any periods that would have been good times to buy stocks? Looking at past and present trends, do you think now is a good time to buy or to sell? Why?

H. Join a Business Explorer Post if there is one in your area. Exploring is open to young men and women aged 14 through 20. To find out about Explorer posts in your area call "Boy Scouts of America" listed in your phone book, and ask for the "Exploring Division."

I. If you are a Boy Scout, try for the American Business and Salesmanship merit badges.

J. If you are a Girl Scout, see if your local troop has the From Dreams to Reality program of career exploration. Troops may also offer opportunities to try out careers through internships, service aide and community action projects, and proficiency badges.

K. Contact the personnel departments of securities firms in your community and ask for career information. Many firms have pamphlets and brochures that describe jobs in the securities industry.

L. For more information on the work of securities sales workers, write to the Security Industry Association, 120 Broadway, New York, NY 10271.

SECURITY SALES WORKER

ACTIVITY 16

Name _____

Class _____

SECURITY SALES WORKER
Related Occupations

Securities sales workers are not the only people who sell relatively expensive items. See if you can unscramble the first four job titles to find four other sales workers whose jobs are similar to the securities sales worker, and the second four job titles to find the some nonselling occupations in the securities industry. Write your answer in the space provided.

1. SUREINCAN GENTA NAD BORRKE
   _____

2. LARE TASTEE TANGE NAD ORBKER.
   _____

3. BILEOOMAUT LASSE ROWREK.
   _____

4. CHATY REKORB.
   _____

5. TIRUCESY STYLANA.
   _____

6. RODER KLERC.
   _____

7. GINMAR RADERT.
   _____

8. DONB DARTER.
   _____

SECURITY SALES WORKER

ACTIVITY 17

Name _____

Class _____

SECURITY SALES WORKER
Math

Consider the stocks listed below. Write your answers in the space provided.

Stock	Price (dollars)	Dividend (dollars per year)
AC&C	60-7/8	4.60
International Computers	263	11.52
American Widget Co.	57	1.90
Fast Food Enterprises	53-3/4	.36
American Railroad Co.	30-1/2	2.32
Mouse Traps Inc.	40-3/4	.32
D.C. Electric Co.	14-5/8	1.34

1. An investor is trying to decide between putting her money in a savings account yielding 5.5 percent per year or investing in a dividend-paying stock.

a. Which of the following stocks would provide a higher yield on her money than the savings account? (Forget about the possibility of capital gains or losses.)

_____
_____
_____
_____
_____
_____

b. Which stocks would provide a higher yield than the savings account?

_____
_____
_____
_____
_____
_____

PARTS COUNTER WORKER

A. Arrange a visit to an auto parts store. Ask the counter worker to show you how to find a specific part in the parts catalog. Then see if you can find the price for the part in the price list. See if the counter worker has any extra or out-of-date catalogs and price lists that you can take home.

B. If you own a bicycle, see how many parts you can identify. You should be able to identify at least 50 parts. Can you imagine how complicated an auto parts counter worker's job is with the thousands of different parts in each car and the hundreds of different types of cars?

C. Join an Auto Mechanic Explorer Post if there is one in your area. Exploring is open to young men and women aged 14 through 20. To find out about Explorer posts in your area, call "Boy Scouts of America" listed in your phone book, and ask for the "Exploring Division."

D. If you are a Boy Scout, try for a merit badge in Salesmanship.

E. Join a chapter of VICA (Vocational Industrial Clubs of America) if your school has one. VICA chapters plan projects, take field trips, and hold competitions in such skill areas as auto mechanics.

F. Join a chapter of DECA (Distributive Education Clubs of America) if your school has one. DECA clubs aid in the development of good sales habits and techniques, and help students get part-time sales jobs while they are still in school.

G. Spend time on hobbies and other activities in which you build or repair things. You might, for example, volunteer to repair appliances for a good cause or make repairs around your house.

H. Participate in an activity that involves handling money and making change. Selling tickets, working in a concession stand during athletic events, selling Girl Scout cookies, or having a newspaper route would all provide good experience.

I. Write for information on a career as a parts counter worker to Automobile Service Industries Association, 444 North Michigan Avenue, Chicago, IL 60611, Automotive Service Association, 1901 Airpoer Fwy., P.O. Box 929, Bedford, TX 76021-0929.

PARTS COUNTER WORKER

ACTIVITY 18

Name _____
Class _____

PARTS COUNTER WORKER
Related Occupations

Parts counter workers are just one line in a chain of automobile-related sales occupations. The work of five other people is described below. If you need to, refer to the list of job titles. Write your answers in the space provided.

Automobile mechanic
Automobile sales worker
Automobile service adviser

Gasoline service station attendant
Manufacturer's representative

1. I work for a company that makes automobile parts and accessories. I visit auto parts stores and sell them the parts my company makes. Who am I?

   _____

2. I work for new and used car dealers. My earnings aren't always as steady as a parts counter worker's, but once I made over $1,000 in 1 week selling new cars. Who am I?

   _____

3. I work for a large automobile dealership. When customers have problems with their cars, I am usually the first person they see. I determine what is wrong with the car, write a repair order, and then get a mechanic to do the actual repair. Who am I?

   _____

4. I'm not actually a sales worker, but I need to know as much about cars and how they work as a parts counter worker does. In fact, cars wouldn't last long if it weren't for me, because I am the person who fixes them when they aren't running well. Who am I?

   _____

5. I also keep cars on the road and trouble free. I put fuel into them and check items such as oil level, tire pressure, and transmission fluid level. I also do minor repairs such as fixing flats. Who am I?

   _____

Exploring Careers—Instructor's Guide   ©1990, JIST Works, Inc., Indianapolis, Indiana

GASOLINE SERVICE STATION ATTENDANT

A. The next time you are in a service station, watch the attendant as he or she services your family car. Ask the attendant to show you how to check the air pressure in the tires. What happens if the tire pressures are not even?

B. Read the owner's manual for your family car (it's probably in the glove compartment). The manual can show a lot about how a car works. Can you understand the manual? Does it interest you?

C. Take part in school, religious, or community activities that involve meeting the public, handling money and making change, and writing out receipts.

D. Ask your parents if you can check the motor oil level in the family car. What happens if the car is driven without enough oil in the motor?

E. Join a chapter of VICA (Vocational Industrial Clubs of America) if your school has one. VICA chapters plan projects, take field trips, and hold competitions in such skill areas as automobile mechanics.

F. Join a chapter of DECA (Distributive Education Clubs of America) if your school has one. DECA clubs aid in the development of good sales habits and techniques, and assist students in obtaining part-time sales jobs while they are still in school.

G. If you are a Boy Scout, try for a merit badge in Salesmanship and Traffic Safety.

H. Join an Auto Mechanic Explorer Post if there is one in your area. Exploring is open to young men and women aged 14 through 20. To find out about Explorer posts in your area, call "Boy Scouts of America" listed in your phone book, and ask for the "Exploring Division."

I. Write to a major oil company and ask for information on becoming a gasoline station attendant or manager.

GASOLINE SERVICE STATION ATTENDANT

ACTIVITY 19

Name _____
Class _____

GASOLINE SERVICE STATION ATTENDANT
Related Occupations

Gasoline service station work offers good opportunities for people who want to work part-time—high school and college students who are unable to hold a full-time job, for example. Fourteen other occupations in which large numbers of students work part-time are described below. Try to match the workers with their job titles. Write your answers in the space provided.

Newspaper vendor	Vehicle washer
Retail trade sales clerk	Dining room attendant
Cashier	Dishwasher
Library clerk	Fountain worker
Messenger	Health trainee
Animal caretaker	Amusement attendant
Stock handler	Usher

1. Diane sells clothes in the men's department of a large department store.
   _____

2. Larry clears the tables of dirty dishes in a downtown restaurant.
   _____

3. Jack washes the dishes after Larry brings them to the restaurant kitchen.
   _____

4. Sue helps a veterinarian feed and care for animals who must stay overnight at the veterinarian's office.
   _____

5. Ann shows moviegoers the way to their seats in a large theater.
   _____

6. Bill makes ice cream sodas in the dining area of a large drug store.
   _____

7. George returns books to their shelves in a public library.
   _____

8. Sarah washes buses for a city bus company.
   _____

Exploring Careers—Instructor's Guide ©1990, JIST Works, Inc., Indianapolis, Indiana

GASOLINE SERVICE STATION ATTENDANT

9. Janet works as a student nurse when not attending classes at nursing school.

   _____

10. Greg sells newspapers and magazines at a stand on Main Street.

    _____

11. Susan works behind the cash register in a large discount store.

    _____

12. Dick operates the Ferris Wheel for a small carnival.

    _____

13. Judy delivers messages and carries articles from office to office in a high rise building.

    _____

14. Mary helps stock the shelves in a supermarket.

    _____

BRICKLAYER

A. Help build an outdoor masonry structure such as a retaining wall or a barbecue pit. Help lay a terrace or patio. Help lay a brick or stone walkway.

B. Invite a bricklayer or stonemason to speak to your class about his or her work. Ask the speaker to bring and explain some of his or her tools.

C. Invite a representative of the local bricklayers' union to speak to your class on apprenticeship opportunities in your community.

D. Invite the instructor of a bricklaying course to speak to your class about training opportunities and job prospects for bricklayers in your community. Most school systems have vocational education programs that offer instruction in the building trades. Courses also are given in community colleges, technical institutes, and trade schools.

E. Join a chapter of VICA (Vocational Industrial Clubs of America), if your school has one. VICA chapters plan projects, take field trips, and hold competitions in such skill areas as bricklaying, carpentry, and the electrical trades.

F. If you are a Girl Scout, see if your local troop has the From Dreams to Reality program for exploring careers. Troops also offer opportunities to test career interests through proficiency badges in a number of areas including Handywoman.

G. If you are a Boy Scout, try for a merit badge in Masonry.

H. As a project for a mathematics class, plan a wall to be built of brick or block. This involves deciding on dimensions, pattern bond, and size of joints.

I. Write for career information to the International Masonry Apprenticeship Trust, 815 15th Street, N.W., Suite 711, Washington, D.C. 20005; Associated General Contractors of America, Inc., 1957 E Street, N.W., Washington, D.C. 20006; and Brick Institute of America, 11490 Commerce Park Dr., Reston, VA 22091.

BRICKLAYER

ACTIVITY 20

Name _____

Class _____

BRICKLAYER
Related Occupations

Bricklayers aren't the only construction workers who build structures or surfaces using bricks, stones, concrete, mortar, or cement. Can you identify some of the related occupations described below? If you need help, refer to the list of job titles. Write your answers in the space provided.

Terrazzo Worker
Cement mason
Marble setter

Hod carrier or mason tender
Stonemason
Tilesetter

1. I spread, smooth, and finish poured concrete surfaces. Who am I?

   _____

2. I cut and shape tiles and apply them to walls, floors, ceilings, and roofs. Who am I?

   _____

3. I apply cement, sand, pigment, and marble chips to floors, stairways, and cabinet fixtures to create durable and decorative surfaces. Who am I?

   _____

4. I build stone structures such as piers or walls. I also lay walks, or special types of masonry. Who am I?

   _____

5. I carry bricks, concrete, mortar, or plaster to bricklayers, plasterers, or stonemasons. I also mix mortar by hand or with a mixing machine. Who am I?

   _____

6. I cut and set slabs of marble in floors and walls of buildings. I also polish and repair slabs that already are in place. Who am I?

   _____

BRICKLAYER

ACTIVITY 21

Name _____
Class _____

BRICKLAYER
Math

Bricklayers need a working knowledge of mathematics. They need to be able to take measurements and do calculations. See if you can do the problems below. They are typical of some of the problems bricklayers deal with every day. Write your answers in the space provided.

1. A bricklayer is planning to build a wall using standard size bricks that are 8 inches long, 4 inches wide, and 2-1/4 inches high. There will be a 1/2 inch of mortar between each brick. How long a course can she build with a load of 25 bricks?

   _____

2. A bricklayer lays 80 bricks per hour. How many hours does it take him to lay 960 bricks? How many 8-hour days is that?

   _____

3. A bricklayer is planning a wall that is to be 10 feet high and 40 feet long. If seven bricks equal 1 square foot of wall, estimate the number of bricks the job will require if you allow 10 percent for waste.

   _____

4. A bricklayer requires 5/8 of a cubic yard of mortar to lay 1,000 bricks with 1/2-inch mortar joints. Assume that seven bricks equal 1 square foot. How many cubic yards of mortar are needed to build a wall 200 feet long and 10 feet high?

   _____

Exploring Careers—Instructor's Guide ©1990, JIST Works, Inc., Indianapolis, Indiana

CARPENTER

A. Build a doghouse or birdhouse. Build a bookcase, table, or other piece of furniture.

B. Build the props for a school theatrical production.

C. Volunteer to repair toys at a day care center, Head Start program, or nursery school.

D. Offer to do minor home repairs or help winterize the homes of elderly neighbors. There may be a program of this kind in your community to which you could volunteer your services. To find out, call the local voluntary action center or agency on aging.

E. Help renovate a room or building for a teen club or community center.

F. Invite a carpenter or cabinetmaker to speak to your class about his or her work. Ask the speaker to bring and explain some of his or her tools.

G. Invite the instructor of a carpentry course to speak to your class about training opportunities and job prospects in your community. Most school systems have vocational education programs that offer instruction in the building trades. Courses are given in community colleges, technical institutes, and trade schools.

H. Join a chapter of VICA (Vocational Industrial Clubs of America), if your school has one. VICA chapters plan projects, take field trips, and hold competitions in such skill areas as carpentry, bricklaying, plumbing, and the electrical trades.

I. Invite a representative of the local carpenter's union to speak to your class about apprenticeship opportunities in your community.

J. Invite a woman carpenter to speak to your class about her job and how she got started in the field.

K. If you are a Girl Scout, see if your local troop has the From Dreams to Reality program for exploring careers. Troops also offer opportunities to test career interests through proficiency badges in a number of areas including Handywoman.

L. If you are a Boy Scout, try for the Home Repair merit badge.

M. Use the topic of metrics in woodworking for a report in a mathematics class. You might begin your research by writing for information to the Office of Weights and Measures, National Bureau of Standards, Washington, D.C. 20234. They also will supply a list, by State, of speakers who are willing to talk to groups about the metric system.

N. Write for career information to the Associated General Contractors of America, Inc., 1957 E Street, N.W., Washington, D.C. 20006 and to the United Brotherhood of Carpenters and Joiners of America, 101 Constitution Avenue, N.W., Washington, D.C. 20001.

CARPENTER

ACTIVITY 22

Name _____
Class _____

CARPENTER
Related Occupations

Carpenters are the largest group of building trade workers, and are employed in almost every type of construction activity. A wide variety of jobs are performed by people with different types of carpentry skills and different job titles. To learn more about some of them, match each occupation with the correct description of the objects on which such workers work. Write your answers in the space provided.

Acoustical carpenter **Finish carpenter**
Rough carpenter **Framing carpenter**
Carpet layer **Drywall Installer**
Cabinetmaker

1. Interior and exterior trim, stairs, hardwood floors.
   _____

2. Drywall and other wallboard for ceilings and walls.
   _____

3. Frames of buildings, general carpentry work in residential construction.
   _____

4. Acoustical tile for walls and ceilings.
   _____

5. Concrete forms, scaffolds, temporary frame shelters.
   _____

6. Wooden store fixtures, office equipment, cabinets, and high-grade furniture.
   _____

7. Carpeting installations.
   _____

CARPENTER

ACTIVITY 23

Name _____

Class _____

CARPENTER
Math

Carpenters need a working knowledge of mathematics. They need to be able to take measurements and do calculations. See if you can do the problems below. They are typical of some of the problems carpenters might deal with. Write your answers in the space provided.

1. A carpenter must use an auger bit to drill a hole exactly 5/8 of an inch deep. The bit advances 1/16 of an inch for each turn. How many turns are needed to drill the hole?

   _____

2. A carpenter must place flooring on a concrete slab that is 8 feet by 15 feet. She will be using pine flooring boards that are sold as 1" x 4" x 8'. The carpenter knows, however, that as a result of planing, boards this size are actually 3/4" x 3-3/4" x 8'. How many boards will she need for the job?

   _____

3. An 8-inch-wide rough board is finished by planing 7/8 inch off one side and 3/4 inch off the other side. What is the width of the finished board?

   _____

4. A carpenter is estimating the amount of time required to do a roofing job. He estimates the job will require 20,000 tiles and he knows he can install 1,000 tiles in 1 hour and 45 minutes. How many 8-hour days will be required to complete the job?

   _____

PLUMBER

A. Help with minor plumbing repairs at home. Help your parents replace a washer in a leaky faucet or clean out a sink trap. Your public library has books on home repairs that can guide you.

B. If there is a home repair or winterization program in your community, volunteer to assist one of the plumbers. To find out if there is such a program where you live, check with your local voluntary action center or agency on aging.

C. Help family and friends with automobile engine repairs. Do your own repair work for your bicycle. Mechanical work of this kind will give you practice working with small handtools.

D. Invite a plumber to speak to your class about his or her job. Ask the speaker to bring and explain such tools as wrenches, reamers, drills, braces, and bits.

E. Invite the instructor of a plumbing course to speak to your class about training opportunities and job prospects in your community. Many school systems have vocational education programs that offer instruction in the building trades. Courses also are given in community colleges, technical institutes, and trade schools.

F. Join a chapter of VICA (Vocational Industrial Clubs of America), if your school has one. VICA chapters plan projects, take field trips, and hold competitions in such skill areas as plumbing, carpentry, bricklaying, and the electrical trades.

G. Invite a representative of the local plumbers' union to speak to your class about apprenticeship opportunities in your community.

H. If you are a Girl Scout, see if your troop has the From Dreams to Reality program of career exploration. Troops also offer opportunities to test career interests through proficiency badges in a number of areas including Handywoman.

I. If you are a Boy Scout, try for the Plumbing and Home Repair merit badges.

J. Write for career information to the National Association of Plumbing-Heating-Cooling Contractors, 180 S. Washington St., Falls Church, VA 22046.

PLUMBER

ACTIVITY 24

Name _____
Class _____

PLUMBER
Related Occupations

Plumbers aren't the only skilled workers who deal with metal piping or duct systems. Which plumbing-related occupations are defined below? Unscramble the letters to find out.

1. **RAI NOGITCINODNI, TEGERONARIRIF NDA NTEGIAH HCIEACMN.** I install, service, and repair air-conditioning, heating, and refrigeration and cooling systems.

   _____

2. **DEWRLE.** I join metal parts together using arc or gas welding equipment. I follow layouts, diagrams, work orders, or oral instructions.

   _____

3. **TEHES TEAML KROEWR.** I make, put together, install, and repair sheet-metal products and equipment such as ventilators, control boxes, and furnace casings. I follow work orders or blueprints.

   _____

4. **RTWAE NTARETMTE LNAPT ARTOEPRO.** I control machinery that purifies and clarifies water for human consumption and for industrial use.

   _____

5. **KRNIPESLR TETIFR.** I install, service, and repair the piping and fixtures used in fire sprinkler systems, including hydrants, pumps, and sprinkler head connections.

   _____

PLUMBER

ACTIVITY 25

Name _____

Class _____

PLUMBER
Math

Mathematics is an important tool of the trade for plumbers. They must be able to take measurements and do calculations. See if you can do the problems below. They are typical of some of the problems plumbers might deal with. Write your answers in the space provided.

1. The water pressure in a main supplying an irrigation system is 68 pounds per square inch. If the pressure at the nozzle is 3/8 of the main pressure, what is the pressure at the nozzle?

   _____

2. A plumber cuts the following lengths from a 40-foot piece of pipe: 6-3/4 feet, 4-1/6 feet, 7-1/2 feet, 2-2/3 feet, 5-5/12 feet. How much pipe is left?

   _____

3. The weight of a pipe is directly proportional to its length. If a pipe 8 feet 4 inches long weighs 75 pounds, how much does a pipe 6 feet 8 inches long weigh?

   _____

4. A house drain has a run of 40 feet at a grade of 1/8 inch per foot. The low end has an elevation of 96.25 feet. What elevation is the high end?

   _____

5. Water weighs nearly 8-1/3 pounds per gallon. A gallon equals 231 cubic inches. How many gallons of water are there in a full tank with a volume of 2,079 cubic inches, and how much does this water weigh?

   _____

Exploring Careers—Instructor's Guide ©1990, JIST Works, Inc., Indianapolis, Indiana

AIR TRAFFIC CONTROLLER

A. Join the Civil Air Patrol. This organization, supported by the Air Force, exists in every state. Membership is open to those who are at least 13 years old. The Civil Air Patrol offers its members the opportunity to fly and to learn about the aerospace industry. Some of the subjects studied are navigation, aerodynamics, and electronics. For more information, call the "Civil Air Patrol" listed in your phone book.

B. Join a Transportation or Aerospace Explorer Post if there is one in your area. Exploring is open to young men and women aged 14 through 20. To find out about Explorer posts in your area, call "Boy Scouts of America" listed in your phone book, and ask for the "Exploring Division."

C. If you are a Boy Scout, try for merit badges in Aviation, Communications, and Weather.

D. If you are a Girl Scout, see if your local troop has the From Dreams to Reality program of career exploration. Troops also offer opportunities to try out careers through internships and service aide and community action projects, and proficiency badges in a number of areas including Aviation and Weather.

E. Ask your teacher to talk to the manager of your local airport and arrange for a class tour of the airport.

F. Prepare a report for a science class on the differences between an airport traffic controller (who guides planes in and out of the airport) and an en route controller (who keeps track of planes between airports).

G. Try to increase your ability to observe and remember details. Some things you can do include recalling people's names and phone numbers and playing cards.

H. Prepare a report for your science class on the kinds of weather conditions that permit or cancel a flight. Bring in and explain a flight weather chart.

I. Spend time on hobbies in which you learn about aviation. Some activities include building model airplanes, reading and aviation, and taking flying lessons. Learn the characteristics of different planes.

J. Prepare a report on the history of air travel for a social studies class.

K. Become familiar with electronic communications equipment. Become a ham radio operator. Learn how radar works.

L. What sort of follow-up occurs after a plane crash? Use this topic for a report in a science or social studies class. You might begin your research in the library. You also can write for information to government agencies such as the Civil Aeronautics Board and the Federal Aviation Administration. Officials of your local airport may be willing to talk to you or come and talk to your class about how they investigate plane crashes.

AIR TRAFFIC CONTROLLER

ACTIVITY 26

Name _____

Class _____

AIR TRAFFIC CONTROLLER
Related Occupations

The air traffic controller is one of a team of workers in the sky and on the ground who follow each plane from takeoff to landing. They ensure a safe, smooth flight. Below are 13 of these occupations. See how many of them you can unscramble. Write your answers in the space provided.

1. PLAENARI CHINMAEC
   _____

2. PLAENARI NTAIEMNNCEA REWC
   _____

3. GGABGEA NAERLDH
   _____

4. POICTLO
   _____

5. DIPATSCHRE
   _____

6. CEETCILSRON TCHCINIANE
   _____

7. NE TOURE TFFAICR CLLERONRTO
   _____

8. GHLIFT TTEANADNT
   _____

9. GHLIFT GIEENREN
   _____

10. SSEGNERPA GEANT
    _____

11. TOIPL
    _____

12. SERVEARITON NGAET
    _____

13. CKTEIT NGAET
    _____

RAILROAD PASSENGER CONDUCTOR

A. Take a train ride if there is a railroad line in your town. If the train is not very crowded, talk to the conductor about the work.

B. Find out the difference between a passenger train conductor and a freight train conductor.

C. To get experience in handling money and selling tickets, volunteer to sell tickets at a school play or dance.

D. Role-play a passenger conductor on a commuter run. Include some common situations, such as a passenger who needs scheduling information and a passenger who doesn't have enough money for the fare.

E. Join a Transportation Explorer Post if there is one in your area. Exploring is open to young men and women aged 14 through 20. To find out about Explorer posts in your area, call "Boy Scouts of America" listed in your phone book, and ask for the "Exploring Division."

F. Write for information on careers in railroading to the Association of American Railroads, American Railroads Building, 50 F Street, N.W., Washington, D.C. 20001.

RAILROAD PASSENGER CONDUCTOR

ACTIVITY 27

Name _____

Class _____

RAILROAD PASSENGER CONDUCTOR
Related Occupations

Besides the conductor, many others work to ensure that the train runs safely and smoothly. Hidden in the puzzle below are 15 of these occupations. See how many you can find. The words may be forwards or backwards, either horizontal or vertical. Shade or circle each answer as you find it.

- Blacksmiths
- Boilermakers
- Brake Operator
- Car Repairers
- Dispatcher
- Electrical Workers
- Engineer
- Machinists
- Sheet Metal Workers
- Signal Installers
- Signal Maintainers
- Station Agents
- Telegraphers
- Tower Workers
- Track Workers

E	L	E	C	T	R	I	C	A	L	W	O	R	K	E	R	S	T	E	L	W	E	G
D	B	R	S	R	E	K	A	M	R	E	L	I	O	B	A	L	T	I	M	O	Q	B
E	I	O	H	T	I	B	R	A	K	E	O	P	E	R	A	T	O	R	R	R	D	L
B	W	T	S	E	N	S	R	V	E	S	T	S	I	N	I	H	C	A	M	K	I	A
R	E	E	N	I	G	N	E	H	O	L	L	Y	W	L	S	A	C	K	E	E	S	C
T	E	L	E	G	R	A	P	H	E	R	S	G	A	S	M	I	S	H	I	B	P	K
S	T	A	T	I	O	N	A	G	E	N	T	S	B	A	S	M	I	T	Y	L	A	S
E	Z	G	S	R	E	N	I	A	T	N	I	A	M	L	A	N	G	I	S	A	T	M
A	N	W	T	O	W	E	R	W	O	R	K	E	R	S	O	T	G	N	W	C	C	I
R	Q	G	S	T	A	I	E	N	B	M	A	C	H	P	N	S	V	U	Q	O	H	T
B	E	T	I	L	A	T	R	A	C	K	W	O	R	K	E	R	S	Y	M	R	E	H
E	R	X	K	R	O	W	S	I	G	N	A	L	I	N	S	T	A	L	L	E	R	S
Z	S	H	E	E	T	M	E	T	A	L	W	O	R	K	E	R	S	U	O	Y	P	X

Exploring Careers—Instructor's Guide ©1990, JIST Works, Inc., Indianapolis, Indiana

BUS DRIVER

A. Compare a bus ride through town during rush hour to a ride in the middle of the day. Notice the differences in the amount of traffic, the cost of the trip, the number of passengers, and how long it takes to get from one place to another. What other differences do you observe?

B. Learn to recognize the symbols on road signs and how to follow them.

C. Many people rely on buses to get around town. Buses offer many advantages, including relatively low cost, convenience, and the peace of mind of not having to drive yourself. Other ways to travel around town include cars, bicycles, and taxicabs. Make a list of the advantages and disadvantages of each.

D. Find out what types of bus services are available in your community. You can start by looking in the yellow pages of the telephone book.

E. Invite a representative from a bus company in your area to speak to your class about training requirements and job opportunities for busdrivers in your community. Prepare questions in advance.

F. Learn how to change a flat tire and handle other common repairs on your family car.

G. Learn how to read maps of your city and its surrounding areas. In this way, you can become familiar with the main streets and famous landmarks.

H. To become familiar with handling a motor vehicle, learn how to drive a sit-down power lawnmower, a minibike, or a boat if any of these are available.

I. Join an Auto Mechanics Road Rally, or Transportation Explorer Post if there is one in your area. Exploring is open to young men and women aged 14 through 20. To find out about Explorer posts in your area, call "Boy Scouts of America" listed in your phone book, and ask for the "Exploring Division."

J. Role-play a bus driver on his or her route. Include such common problems as a passenger who does not have enough money for the fare, a passenger who needs information, and a passenger whose conduct is disturbing others on the bus.

BUS DRIVER

ACTIVITY 28

Name _____

Class _____

BUS DRIVER
Related Occupations

See how many of the following workers you can match with their job duties. Like the local transit busdriver, they are all involved in carrying people or goods over our highways and city streets.

Local truckdriver
Route driver
Ambulance driver
Long-distance truckdriver

Chauffeur
Long-distance busdriver
Taxicab driver
School busdriver

1. Transports sick or injured people to the hospital.
   _____

2. Drives a group of passengers from one town to another.
   _____

3. Drives children to school in the morning and back home in the afternoon.
   _____

4. Moves goods from terminals and warehouses to factories, stores, and homes in the area.
   _____

5. Paid and licensed driver of a private motor car.
   _____

6. Delivers goods from the place of business to the customers. May collect payments or try to sell the company's services.
   _____

7. Picks up passengers at any location (often getting the information over a two-way radio) and drives them directly to their destination.
   _____

8. Travels along turnpikes and highways carrying goods between terminals that are thousands of miles apart.
   _____

BIOCHEMIST

A. If you live near a chemical, pharmaceutical, or textile manufacturer, or some other company with a chemical research laboratory, arrange a tour of the lab for your class. Find out what kinds of experiments the scientists perform, what procedures they follow, and what equipment they use.

B. Prepare a report for your science class on one of the following topics:
   - The periodic table of elements. As you read and explore, try to answer these questions: What is an element? How does it differ from a compound? What do the numbers in the table stand for? Why is the table arranged the way it is? (Hint: What do the elements in each column have in common?) Your science teacher and school librarian can suggest books that will help you answer these questions.
   - The elements used in the human body. What elements does your body need to live? How does it take them in? What does it do with them? Make a chart to show how your body obtains and uses oxygen.
   - Animal Cells. Make a drawing of a typical animal cell, labeling all the major parts. What purpose does each part serve? How does an animal cell different from a plant cell? What different kinds of cells are found in the human body?

C. Learn about life science on your own by trying these activities:
   - Keep an aquarium or terrarium.
   - Watch TV specials about wildlife, medicine, and other life science subjects.
   - Check your library for articles of interest in *Science News*, *Scientific American*, and other science journals.
   - Visit nature or wildlife centers in your area. Call the local department of parks and recreation to find these centers.

D. If you are a Boy Scout, try for merit badges in Botany, Zoology, Chemistry, and General Science.

E. If you are a Girl Scout, see if your local troop has the From Dreams to Reality program of career exploration. Troops may also offer opportunities to try out careers through internships, service aide and community action projects, and proficiency badges in a number of areas including Animal Kingdom, Plant Kingdom, and Science.

F. Join a Marine Science, Conservation, or Ecology Explorer Post if there is one in your area. Exploring is open to young men and women aged 14 through 20. To find out about Explorer posts in your area, call "Boy Scouts of America" listed in your phone book, and ask for the "Exploring Division."

G. Invite a biologist, chemist, or biochemist to speak to your class about his or her work. Prepare questions for the speaker in advance.

H. Report to your class on the different kinds of work performed by biologists and chemists. Draw a diagram to show the various branches of each science, describe the work of each branch, and point out where the two sciences overlap. One way to investigate is to write for career information to the American Society of Biological Chemists, 9650 Rockville Pike, Bethesda, Maryland 20814.

BIOCHEMIST

ACTIVITY 29

Name _____
Class _____

BIOCHEMIST
Related Occupations

Biochemists are not the only scientists who deal with living things. Several other kinds of scientists are listed below, along with possible descriptions of what they do. For each occupation, see if you can choose the correct description. Circle the correct answer.

1. **Agronomist**
   a. Improves the quality and yield of agricultural crops.
   b. Studies the different species of spiders.
   c. Performs research on agronomes, which are part of the nucleus of a cell.

2. **Microbiologist**
   a. Develops new ways to use the microscope in biological research.
   b. Breeds plants and animals in order to produce smaller varieties.
   c. Studies the growth and characteristics of bacteria, viruses, and other microscopic organisms.

3. **Pharmacologist**
   a. Investigates the effects of drugs, poisons, and other substances on animals.
   b. Breeds new and better varieties of animals for food.
   c. Decides what medicine each patient in a hospital should receive.

4. **Pathologist**
   a. Studies the migration patterns of animals.
   b. Investigates the effects of diseases, parasites, and insects on human cells, tissues, and organs.
   c. Performs research on the relationship between mental disorders and criminal behavior.

5. **Embryologist**
   a. Studies the causes and effects of genetic defects.
   b. Investigates the development of an animal from fertilization through pregnancy.
   c. Searches for a cure for cancer.

6. **Organic Chemist**
   a. Creates new chemical substances from plants.
   b. Analyzes the chemical processes that take place inside the kidney, liver, and other human organs.
   c. Studies the structure and properties of compounds containing carbon.

7. **Horticulturalist**
   a. Develops new and better methods of cultivating plants for orchards and gardens.
   b. Studies the social structure of bee colonies.
   c. Grows mold cultures in a laboratory in order to make penicillin.

ELECTRICAL ENGINEER

A. Prepare a report on electric power in your community for your science or English class. Describe where and how the electricity you use is generated. Explain how it travels to your home. Explain how the quantity of electricity is measured and how much is used in your area. The community relations department of your local power company may have brochures and pamphlets that you can include in your report.

B. Arrange a class tour of a power station.

C. Prepare a report about electric current for your science class. Explain the difference between alternating and direct current (AC and DC). What kind of current is used in an automobile engine? A flashlight? Your home? How can you tell whether an electric line has AC or DC?

D. Learn about electricity on your own. Look for books on electricity in your school or public library. Some books outline simple experiments you can perform.

E. Experiment with electrical circuits. Hobby shops have kits that you can use to experiment with different kinds of simple circuits. Learn how to draw a diagram of a circuit. Find out what each symbol stands for.

F. Prepare a report for your science class about home appliances that use electricity. Which are electric? What do the electric appliances have in common? Explain why some appliance plugs have two prongs, while others have three. What is the purpose of the third prong?

G. Ask your parents to show you the fusebox or circuit breaker panel in your home. Find out why it is needed and what to do if a fuse or circuit breaker pops.

H. Build a crystal radio set. You can get help from books at your school or public library.

I. Become a ham radio operator. (Ham radios should not be confused with citizen's band, or CB, radios. With CB you can communicate only by voice and only over short distances. With a ham radio you use Morse code as well as voice, and you can broadcast all over the world.) To get your first license, you must demonstrate knowledge of radio concepts and the ability to understand Morse code at the rate of 5 words per minute. For full information, write to the American Radio Relay League, 225 Main Street, Newington, CT 06111.

J. Invite an electrical engineer to speak to your class about his or her job.

K. If you are a Boy Scout, try for merit badges in Electronics and Engineering.

L. If you are a Girl Scout, see if your local troop has the From Dreams to Reality program of career exploration. Troops also offer opportunities to test career interests through proficiency badges in a number of areas such as Science.

M. Join an Electronics or Engineering Explorer Post if there is one in your area. Exploring is open to young men and women aged 14 through 20. To find out about Explorer posts in your area, call "Boy Scouts of America" listed in your phone book, and ask for the "Explorer Division."

N. Enter a project on electronics in a science fair.

O. Visit a museum with your science class. Concentrate on the exhibits on electronics, computers, aviation, and space travel. Prepare questions for the museum guide on the contributions engineers have made in these areas.

P. To see if you can think abstractly, like an engineer, play mental tic-tac-toe. Picture the board in your mind, with each square numbered, one through nine. Play each turn by saying out loud the number of the square you want to mark. If one player forgets and names an occupied square, the other player wins. You'll have to concentrate to remember all the plays. It's harder than it sounds!

Q. Write for the pamphlet on careers put out by the Educational Services Department, Institute of Electrical and Electronics Engineers, 1111 19th St., N.W., Suite 608, Washington, D.C. 20036.

ELECTRICAL ENGINEER

ACTIVITY 30

Name _____

Class _____

ELECTRICAL ENGINEER
Related Occupations

Many kinds of engineers design, develop, and test products or systems. Electrical engineers are one kind. The names of ten others are listed below in jumbled form. See if you can figure out what they are. To help you, next to each name there are examples of the products or systems that the engineer works on. Write your answers in the space provided.

1. AIRMEN (Steam engines for ships)
   _____

2. ANCHEMICAL (Air-conditioning systems)
   _____

3. CANRULE (Atomic reactors)
   _____

4. CAUREALATION (Airplanes and rockets)
   _____

5. CEMICAR (Glass and tile)
   _____

6. CIMLEACH (Rubber and plastics)
   _____

7. ILVIC (Bridges, dams, and roads)
   _____

8. PARTNATIONSORT (Streets and highways)
   _____

9. TOOTUMIVEA (Car and truck motors)
   _____

10. TOPICAL (Telescopes and cameras)
    _____

Exploring Careers—Instructor's Guide ©1990 JIST Works, Inc., Indianapolis, Indiana

BROADCAST TECHNICIAN

A. Arrange a tour of a radio or TV station for yourself or your class. Prepare questions for the employees about their work.

B. Listen to the radio. Pick out the recorded voices (such as repeated commercials and jingles) from the live voices (disc jockeys and news announcers). Try to imagine how the recordings were made and how they are played during the program. This activity may be easier after doing the preceding one.

C. Listen to AM radio at two different times of day, once during daylight (say, 4 p.m.) and once after dark (say, 9 p.m.). Each time pick a dozen or so stations listing the call letters (such as WDAD or KMOM), location, and, if possible, frequency (number on the dial) of each. Do you notice a difference between the two lists? The stations on the daytime list are likely to be broadcasting from a much shorter distance away than those on the night list. Investigate the reason for this.

D. Build a crystal radio set. You can get help from books at your school or public library.

E. Become a ham radio operator (Ham radios should not be confused with citizen's band, or CB, radios. With CB you can communicate only by voice and only over short distances. With a ham radio you use Morse code as well as voice, and you can broadcast all over the world.) To get your first license, you must demonstrate knowledge of radio concepts and the ability to understand Morse code at the rate of 5 words per minute. For full information, write to the American Radio Relay League, 225 Main Street, Newington, CT 06111.

F. Prepare a report for your science class. Answer the following questions in your report: What do AM and FM stand for? What is the difference between the two? What are the advantages of each? How and when did each come into existence? What are some of the other bands, and how are they used? Include in your report a diagram and an explanation of how sound travels from a source to the listener's radio.

G. If you are a Girl Scout, see if your local troop has the From Dreams to Reality program of career exploration. Troops may also offer opportunities to test career interests through proficiency badges in a number of areas including Radio and Television.

H. If you are a Boy Scout, try for merit badges in Communications, Electronics, Public Speaking, and Radio.

I. Join a Broadcasting, Electronics, Amateur Radio, or Communications Explorer Post if there is one in your area. Exploring is open to young men and women aged 14 through 20. To find out about Explorer posts in your area, call "Boy Scouts of America" listed in your phone book, and ask for the "Exploring Division."

J. Write for information on careers to the National Association of Broadcasters, 1771 N Street, N.W., Washington, D.C. 20036 or to the Corporation for Public Broadcasting, 1111 16th Street, N.W., Washington, D.C. 20036. For information on the Radiotelephone Operator's License, write to the Consumer Assistance Office, Federal Communications Commission, 1919 M Street, N.W., Washington, D.C. 20554. For information on technical careers, write to Technical Careers, Box 111, Washington, D.C. 20044.

AUTO MECHANIC

A. Read about cars. Your school or public library has books about automobiles and automotive repair. Newsstands often have magazines about cars. The owner's manual for your family car lists its service requirements. If some of these books and magazines are too technical to understand at first, don't become discouraged; many pamphlets are written for people without technical training. For example, you can write to the Consumer Information Center, Pueblo, Colorado 81009 to get the Federal Government's Consumer Information Catalog. Some of the booklets listed there tell how to recognize common car problems, change motor oil, and do a basic engine tune-up.

B. Use school assignments to learn about cars. You might build a model of a gasoline engine for a science fair. Or write a report about different kinds of engines for an English or a science class.

C. The conversion to the metric system will affect the work of automobile mechanics. Mechanics will have to use different units of measurement for many items such as engine power (kilowatts rather than horsepower), tire pressure (kilopascals rather than pounds per square inch), and gasoline consumption (liters per 100 kilometers rather than miles per gallon). Automobile mechanics who repair foreign cars already use some metric measurements.

D. Use the topic of metric measurements in automobile servicing for a report in a mathematics class. You might begin your research by writing for information to the Office of Weights and Measures, National Bureau of Standards, Washington, D.C. 20234. That office also will supply a list, by State, of speakers who are willing to talk to groups about the metric system.

E. Look for opportunities to repair machines. Work with relatives and friends who repair or service cars, bicycles, or other machines.

F. If there are automobile or bicycle repair clinics in your community, attend them. These clinics give you a chance to learn basic repairs, such as changing tires.

G. Join an Automotive Explorer Post if there is one in your area. Exploring is open to young men and women aged 14 through 20. To find out about Explorer posts in your area, call "Boy Scouts of America" listed in your phone book, and ask for the "Exploring Division."

H. Find out if your school system has courses in auto mechanics. Ask the instructor to come and speak to your class.

I. Join a chapter of VICA (Vocational Industrial Clubs of America) if your school has one. VICA chapters plan projects, take field trips, and hold competitions in such skill areas as auto mechanics, auto body, and diesel mechanics.

J. Work with your hands and use tools. Find out what tools you have in your home that mechanics use. Learn to use these tools. Repair and service your bicycle or old machinery such as a typewriter or a clock.

K. Arrange a class tour of a service department of an automobile dealership. Note that each mechanic may specialize in one type of repair. There may be a brake repairer, a carburetor mechanic, a front-end mechanic, a transmission mechanic, a tune-up mechanic, and a rattle, squeak, and leak mechanic.

L. Role-play a conversation between a mechanic and a customer. Pretend that you are the mechanic and ask one of your classmates to play the part of the customer. Explain an automotive repair as references.

AUTO MECHANIC

ACTIVITY 31

Name _____
Class _____

AUTO MECHANIC
Related Occupations

Would you like to keep engines running and wheels rolling? Repairing automobiles is just one way of doing it. Unscramble the words listed below to find the names of other mechanics who work with gasoline engines or vehicles.

1. FABRICRAT INAHMCCE
   _____

2. LBCYCIE ERIARRPE
   _____

3. OTAB NEENIG INAHMCCE
   _____

4. USB INAHMCCE
   _____

5. LSDEIE INAHMCCE
   _____

6. AMRF NEUIQPTME INAHMCCE
   _____

7. YECLROOTMC INAHMCCE
   _____

8. SALML ENNIGE INAHMCCE
   _____

9. KTUCR INAHMCCE
   _____

6. AMRF NEUIQPTME INAHMCCE
   _____

7. YECLROOTMC INAHMCCE
   _____

8. SALML ENNIGE INAHMCCE
   _____

9. KTUCR INAHMCCE
   _____

COMPUTER SERVICE TECHNICIAN

A. Use class assignments to learn more about computers. You might do a project on electronics or computers for a science fair. Or prepare a report on electricity, electronics, or computers for a science or English class. Your library has books that can help you.

B. Arrange to have a computer service technician speak to your class.

C. Look for an electronic hobby kit in a hobby shop or department store. Visit a computer store if there is one in your area. Build a small computer from a kit.

D. Build a crystal radio set. You can get help from books in your school or public library.

E. Join a Computer or an Electronics Explorer Post if there is one in your area. Exploring is open to young men and women aged 14 through 20. To find out about Explorer posts in your area, call "Boy Scouts of America" listed in your phone book, and ask for the "Exploring Division."

F. If you are a Girl Scout, see if your troop has the From Dreams to Reality program of career exploration. Scouts learn about electronics and machine repair through site visits, speakers, and actual experience.

G. If you are a Boy Scout, try for Computer, Electricity, Electronics, Machinery, or Radio merit badges.

H. Join a chapter of VICA (Vocational Industrial Clubs of America) if your school has one. VICA chapters plan projects, take field trips, and hold competitions in such skill areas as industrial electronics, electrical trades, and radio and TV repair.

I. Dealing with people is an important part of a technician's work. Try tutoring other students in mathematics or science to gain experience explaining problems.

COMPUTER SERVICE TECHNICIAN

ACTIVITY 32

Name _____
Class _____

COMPUTER SERVICE TECHNICIAN
Related Occupations

Computer service technicians aren't the only mechanics who fix electronic machinery. Decode the words below to find others. Each number stands for a letter. Use these clues to get started. Write your answers in the space provided.

1 = A
9 = I
21 = U

5 = E
15 = O
25 = Y

1. 1-16-16-12-9-1-14-3-5 18-5-16-1-9-18-5-18
   _____

2. 1-21-20-15-13-15-20-9-22-5
   5-12-5-3-20-18-9-3-9-1-14
   _____

3. 2-21-19-9-14-5-19-19 13-1-3-8-9-14-5
   13-5-3-8-1-14-9-3
   _____

4. 5-12-5-3-20-18-15-14-9-3 15-18-7-1-14
   20-5-3-8-14-9-3-9-1-14
   _____

5. 9-14-19-20-18-21-13-5-14-20
   18-5-16-1-9-18-5-18
   _____

6. 18-1-4-9-15 18-5-16-1-9-18-5-18
   _____

7. 18-1-4-1-18 13-5-3-8-1-14-9-3
   _____

8. 20-22 19-5-18-22-9-3-5 20-5-3-8-14-9-3-9-1-14
   _____

JEWELER

A. Use jewelry and jewelry making as topics for school assignments. Write about jewelry styles during different periods of history for an English or social studies report. Design or make jewelry for an art class. Explain or demonstrate how jewelry is electroplated for a science class. For a mathematics class, prepare a report on the systems of measurements used by jewelers—karats and troy weight for gems and carats for precious metals. Your library has books that will help you with these projects.

B. Visit exhibits of jewelry in museums, shopping malls, and craft fairs. Look for an opportunity to talk with goldsmiths, silversmiths, enamelists, or other craft workers who make jewelry or works of art from precious metals or stones. Ask about their work. How do they feel about it? How did they become interested in their craft? How did they learn their skills?

C. Arrange a class tour of a jewelry repair shop or a jewelry store that has a jeweler. If there is a jewelry factory in your area, try to arrange a class tour. You will see that the work in the jewelry factory is much more specialized than in a store or repair shop.

D. Make some jewelry. Learn what tools jewelers use; learn how they shape metal. You will find jewelry kits in hobby shops and department stores. These can help you learn basic manual skills. Look for kits that use metal or involve very detailed and delicate work. Other activities that will help you develop manual skills are model building and needlework.

E. If you are a Girl Scout, see if your local troop has the From Dreams to Reality program of career exploration. Troops also may offer opportunities to try out careers through internships, service aide and community action projects, and proficiency badges in a number of areas including Ceramics and Pottery and Metal Arts.

F. If you are a Boy Scout, try for merit badges in Drafting, Leatherwork, Machinery, Metalwork, Model Design and Building, Pottery, or Sculpture.

G. Join a chapter of VICA (Vocational Industrial Clubs of America) if your school has one. VICA chapters plan projects, take field trips, and hold competitions in such skill areas as jewelry repair and watchmaking.

H. Write for information about the occupation to Retail Jewelers of America, Time-Life Building, Rockefeller Center, 1271 Avenue of the Americas, New York, NY 10020.

JEWELER

ACTIVITY 33

Name _____
Class _____

JEWELER
Related Occupations

Jewelers are not the only workers who make and repair metal products. Descriptions of seven such workers are listed below, along with the names of seven occupations. Try to match the workers with their job titles. Write your answers in the space provided.

Automobile Body Repairer **Goldsmith**
Machinist **Modelmaker**
Silversmith **Tool Maker**
Watch Repairer

1. Max uses hammers, torches and crowbars to make accident cases look like new.
   _____

2. Neal makes parts for cars, ships, trains, and other machines. He uses lathes, milling machines, and other power tools and works with many different metals, including steel, iron, aluminum, and brass.
   _____

3. Hope makes metal samples that are used to mass produce jewelry. She shapes metals such as brass just as a jeweler shapes gold, silver, or platinum.
   _____

4. Emily works from sketches and diagrams just like a jeweler. She makes the part of a lathe, milling machine, or other machine tool that cuts metal.
   _____

5. Phil uses a precious metal to make and repair jewelry, knives, forks, plates, and tea sets.
   _____

6. Karen specializes in making and repairing jewelry from one precious metal.
   _____

7. Because Larry often wears magnifying glasses on the job, many people think he is a jeweler. Actually, he repairs one of the smallest and most commonly used machines.
   _____

REGISTERED NURSE

A. Volunteer to work in a hospital, nursing home, or clinic in your community. Volunteers typically provide entertainment; deliver mail and flowers to patients; write letters for patients and read to them; visit patients to cheer them up; run errands; direct visitors; conduct play activities for children; and provide baby-sitting services for visitors. The also do clerical jobs such as typing, filing, and stuffing envelopes.

B. Get in touch with the American National Red Cross about opportunities to work as a youth volunteer. Red Cross youth volunteers serve as tutors for younger children and as aides in hospitals, day care centers, and nursing homes; recruit blood donors; help with programs to combat drug abuse among young people; and play and study with homebound and handicapped children.

C. Contact the Boys' Club or Girls' Club in your community. Clubs offer a wide variety of programs including volunteer service at hospitals and work with retarded and handicapped children.

D. Baby-sit for a younger brother or sister. Take care of a neighbor's child. How does it feel to have someone depend on you?

E. Care for neighbors' pets when the owners go away. You'll have the experience of being responsible for an animal's basic needs.

F. Ask your teacher to arrange a class tour of a hospital or nursing home.

G. Invite one or more nurses to speak to your class about their jobs. Ask the speakers to discuss their duties, their training, and the rewards and frustrations of nursing. If possible, arrange for a panel discussion by nurses in several different specialties: A school nurse, a psychiatric nurse, a public health nurse, and an emergency room nurse, for example.

H. Contact your local chapter of the American National Red Cross to arrange a demonstration, talk, or movie on first aid for your science or health class.

I. Take a course in first aid from a certified instructor. First-aid courses teach you how to prevent accidents; how to protect accident victims; how to give emergency care for severe bleeding, stoppage of breathing, or oral poisoning; and how to take care of minor injuries.

J. Ask the school nurse to teach you how to take someone's pulse, blood pressure, and temperature.

K. Join a Science Club or a Health Career Club if there is one in your school.

L. Use nursing as a topic for class assignments. Read a biography of Florence Nightingale for a book report in an English class. Prepare a report on the history of nursing for a social studies class. Explore an issue in public health, such as pollution, smoking, or drug abuse, for a science or health class. Choose a topic in biology or medicine for a science fair project. Report on metric measurements in the health field for a mathematics class.

M. Use first aid as a topic for a report in a science or health class.
- Describe what should be done for severe bleeding. When should a tourniquet be used?
- Explain the dangers of moving a seriously injured person. Tell how you would decide what method to use. Demonstrate a chair carry and a two-person carry. Show how to improvise and use a stretcher.
- Demonstrate how to apply an adhesive bandage, a large gauze compress held in place by tape, a dressing on the eye with a cravat, and a roller bandage on the ankle and foot, wrist and hand, forearm, and finger.

REGISTERED NURSE

- Explain how to recognize and treat unconsciousness, shock, convulsions, poisoning by mouth, burns, and injuries to joints.
- Explain the objectives of artificial respiration. Demonstrate mouth-to-mouth and mouth-to-nose rescue breathing as well as the chest-pressure armlift and back-pressure arm-lift.
- Explain cardiopulmonary resuscitation (CPR).

N. Take a course in lifesaving from a certified organization. The Red Cross and the Boy Scouts of America both offer courses in Junior Lifesaving.

O. Join an Explorer Post if there is one in your area. Exploring, open to young men and women aged 14 through 20, offers programs in nursing, medicine and health careers, physical or natural science, child care, and emergency first aid. To find out about Explorer posts in your community, call "Boy Scouts of America" listed in your phone book, and ask for the "Exploring Division."

P. If you are a Boy Scout, earn a merit badge in Public Health, First Aid, General Science, Lifesaving, or Emergency Preparedness.

Q. If you are a Girl Scout, see if your local troop has the From Dreams to Reality program for exploring careers. Troops also sponsor service aide and community action projects in the health field, and offer proficiency badges in First Aid, Nursing, Lifesaving, Public Health, and Science.

R. Write for career information to the National League for Nursing, Career Information Services, 10 Columbus Circle, New York, NY 10019, and to the Nurses Organization of the Veterans Administration, 6728 Old McLean Village Dr., McLean, VA 22101.

REGISTERED NURSE

ACTIVITY 34

Name _____
Class _____

REGISTERED NURSE
Related Occupations

Registered nurses work in many different settings. Some of these are listed below. Choose the statement that applies to each nurse's specialty. Circle the letter of each correct statement.

1. **School nurse**
   a. Finds cures for contagious diseases peculiar to children
   b. Gives immunizations and maintains students' health records
   c. Teaches in a school of nursing

2. **Public health nurse**
   a. Prescribes medication for acne
   b. Writes advertisements for drug companies
   c. Teaches neighborhood residents about nutrition, hygiene, and other aspects of good health

3. **Nurse-midwife**
   a. Works under the supervision of a cardiologist
   b. Delivers babies and teaches new mothers sound health practices.
   c. Trains ambulance personnel

4. **Nurse anesthetist**
   a. Administers drugs so that patients don't feel pain during operations or childbirth.
   b. Examines ears, nose, and throat for signs of disease
   c. Develops vaccines for protection against disease

5. **Office nurse**
   a. Prepares a physician's patients for examination and provides whatever help the physician needs
   b. Gives first aid to office employees
   c. Tests for the presence of bacteria in a community water supply

6. **Private duty nurse**
   a. Plans nutritious meals for hospital patients
   b. Provides nursing care, for a fee, in the patient's home or in a hospital or nursing home.
   c. Operates an artificial kidney machine

7. **Occupational health or industrial nurse**
   a. Teaches blind patients new job skills
   b. Directs research to protect industrial workers from radiation hazards
   c. Treats employees and customers who become ill or have an accident in a department store, factory, or other business firm.

8. **Psychiatric nurse**
   a. Studies the effects of high-altitude flying on airplane pilots.
   b. Cares for patients who are mentally ill
   c. Performs brain surgery

Exploring Careers—Instructor's Guide ©1990, JIST Works, Inc., Indianapolis, Indiana

REGISTERED NURSE

9. **Rehabilitation nurse**
   a. Cares for patients who have chronic or disabling conditions, conditions that can't be cured quickly—if ever
   b. Converts old buildings into nursing homes
   c. Estimates future hospital costs for insurance companies

10. **Consultant nurse**
    a. Organizes volunteer services in a hospital or nursing home.
    b. Sells drugs to hospitals
    c. Advises hospitals and nursing homes on ways to improve their nursing care

MEDICAL TECHNOLOGIST

A. Stimulate your interest in science by reading and doing experiments or projects.
- Work with a chemistry set, the kind available in hobby shops or department stores.
- Prepare slides and examine them under a microscope.
- Do a project in the life sciences for a science fair.
- Read popular science magazines.

B. Join a Science Club or a Health Careers Club if there is one in your school.

C. Contact your local chapter of the American National Red Cross to arrange a talk for your science or health class on the Red Cross blood program.

D. Ask your teacher to arrange a class tour of a medical laboratory.

E. Invite a medical technologist to speak to your class about his or her job. Ask the speaker to bring and explain some of the equipment used in a medical laboratory. Ask him or her to talk about job duties, training, and the rewards and frustrations of this kind of work.

F. Volunteer to work in the medical laboratory of a hospital, clinic, or nursing home. You might be able to run errands, wash equipment, or do clerical work.

G. Get in touch with the American National Red Cross about opportunities to work as a youth volunteer. Red Cross youth volunteers help recruit blood donors, serve as tutors for younger children, and as aides in hospitals, day care centers, and nursing homes.

H. Join an Explorer Post if there is one in your area. Exploring, open to young men and women aged 14 through 20, offers programs in medicine and health careers, physical or natural science, and emergency first aid. To find out about Explorer posts in your community, call "Boy Scouts of America" listed in your phone book, and ask for the "Exploring Division."

I. If you are a Girl Scout, earn a proficiency badge in Science, Public Health, or First Aid.

J. If you are a Boy Scout, earn a merit badge in General Science, Public Health, First Aid, Lifesaving, or Emergency Preparedness.

K. Take a course in first aid from a certified instructor.

L. Prepare a report for a science or health class on the diseases spread by rats, flies, worms, and ticks. Explain how people catch yellow fever, rabies, hookworm, typhoid fever, and tetanus.

M. Write for career information to American Medical Technologists, 710 Higgins Road, Park Ridge, Illinois 60068; American Society for Medical Technology, 2021 L. St., N.W., Suite 400, Washington, D.C. 20036; American Society of Clinical Pathologists, Board of Registry, P.O. Box 12270, Chicago, IL 60612; and International Society for Clinical Laboratory Technology, 818 Olive Street, Suite 918, St. Louis, Missouri 63101.

MEDICAL TECHNOLOGIST

ACTIVITY 35

Name _____
Class _____

MEDICAL TECHNOLOGIST
Related Occupations

Medical technologists aren't the only people whose work in laboratories helps us to understand and treat disease. Ten other occupations are listed below. See if you can choose the correct job duty for each.

1. Medical laboratory technician
   a. prepares patient's medical records
   b. does routine laboratory tests for use in diagnosing or treating disease
   c. mixes drugs under the direction of pharmacist

   _____

2. Veterinary laboratory technician
   a. investigates animal diseases that can be caught by humans
   b. inspects livestock in slaughterhouses
   c. prepares vaccines that protect animals against disease

   _____

3. Medical laboratory assistant
   a. stores and labels plasma and does other routine work in a blood bank
   b. performs autopsies to determine the cause of death
   c. conducts research to protect medical laboratory personnel against infection

   _____

4. Pathologist
   a. runs a machine that does computerized brain scans
   b. studies disease and its effect on the cells and tissues of our bodies
   c. studies insects and their relation to plant life.

   _____

5. Chemist
   a. conducts research and experiments on gaseous, liquid, and solid materials
   b. develops computer programs for drug manufacturers
   c. designs biomedical laboratory equipment

   _____

6. Cytotechnologist
   a. measures radioactivity in the cells of workers at nuclear reactors
   b. studies bee culture and breeding
   c. stains, mounts, and examines human body cells under a microscope

   _____

MEDICAL TECHNOLOGIST

7. Zoologist
   a. designs natural habitats for animals in zoos
   b. studies origin, classification, habits, and diseases of animals
   c. plans breeding studies to improve varieties of plants

8. Histologic technician
   a. prepares sections of body tissues for examination by a pathologist
   b. removes deposits and stains from teeth
   c. operates ultrasound diagnostic equipment to produce pictures of internal organs

9. Biochemist
   a. specializes in taking X-rays of specific parts of the body
   b. measures impulse frequencies from the brain
   c. studies chemical processes of living organisms in order to understand allergies, vitamin deficiency, hormonal imbalance, and other medical problems

10. Geneticist
    a. handles legal problems in the field of inheritance taxes
    b. conducts research on inherited traits such as hair and eye color and resistance to disease
    c. tests blood samples using an automatic blood analyzer

Exploring Careers—Instructor's Guide ©1990, JIST Works, Inc., Indianapolis, Indiana

PHYSICAL THERAPIST

A. Volunteer to work in a hospital, nursing home, or clinic in your community.

B. Look for opportunities to spend time with handicapped or retarded children. Studying and playing with handicapped children will help you develop the natural, accepting manner that physical therapists must have to deal effectively with disabled patients. Girls' Clubs and Boys' Clubs in many communities offer programs including volunteer service at hospitals and work with retarded and handicapped children. Red Cross youth volunteers play and study with homebound and handicapped children. Red Cross youth volunteers play and study with homebound and handicapped children. Scout troops, Campfire Girls, and other youth organizations offer similar opportunities.

C. Ask your teacher to arrange a class tour of the physical therapy department of a local hospital or nursing home.

D. Invite a physical therapist to speak to your class about his or her job. Suggest that the speaker bring some equipment and demonstrate its use. Ask him or her to discuss job duties, training, and the rewards and frustrations of the work.

E. Interview a friend or classmate who has undergone physical therapy. Find out about his or her treatment and relationship with the physical therapist.

F. Help manage a team involved in a contact sport such as football in which bone, muscle, and nerve injuries are common. Observe the kinds of therapy the injured players are undergoing.

G. Take the Junior Life Saving Course offered by the American Red Cross of the Boy Scouts of America, or a course offered by another certified organization.

H. Develop your teaching skills by volunteering to help direct children in sports or arts and crafts at a day care center or summer recreational program.

I. Join an Explorer Post if there is one in your area. Exploring, open to young men and women aged 14 through 20, offers programs in medicine and health careers, physical or natural science, and emergency first aid. To find out about Explorer posts in your area call "Boy Scouts of America" listed in your phone book, and ask for the "Exploring Division."

J. If you are a Girl Scout, earn a proficiency badge in First Aid, Lifesaving, Public Health, or Science.

K. If you are a Boy Scout, earn a merit badge in Personal Fitness, Lifesaving, Emergency Preparedness, Public Health First Aid or General Science.

L. Use the topic of rehabilitation for a report in a science or health class. You might prepare a report, together with charts and other illustrations, that show the muscles of the body and how they interact. Explain how exercises can strengthen various parts of your body such as your arms, shoulders, chest, abdomen, back, or legs.

M. Prepare a report for a health class on what to do for heatstroke, heat exhaustion, frostbite, bruises, and arm and leg cramps.

N. Develop an exercise program to increase your strength, endurance, speed, and coordination. Include calisthenics, running, swimming, jumping, and other activities.

O. Write for career information to the American Physical Therapy Association, 1111 North Fairfax St., Alexandria, VA 22314, and to the Veterans Administration, Department of Medicine and Surgery, 810 Vermont Avenue, N.W., Washington, D.C. 20420.

PHYSICAL THERAPIST

ACTIVITY 36

Name _____
Class _____

PHYSICAL THERAPIST
Related Occupations

Physical therapists are not the only workers involved in therapy and rehabilitation. The duties of other workers in this field are described below. Match these duties with the job titles listed below. Write your answers in the space provided.

Physical therapist assistant or aide
Occupational therapist
Occupational therapy assistant
Speech pathologist or audiologist
Respiratory therapy worker
Recreational therapist
Art therapist

Music therapist
Prosthetist
Chiropractor
Osteopathic physician
Orthopedic surgeon
Dance therapist

1. I teach art to help my patients express their feelings and do something that makes them feel better about themselves. I work with patients in such places as rehabilitation centers and mental hospitals. Who am I?

   _____

2. I design, make, and fit artificial limbs known as prostheses. Who am I?

   _____

3. My patients are mentally or physically disabled. I help them master everyday skills such as shaving, and teach them things like woodworking or gardening that make their day more enjoyable. If I can, I teach them skills that will help them get a job. Who am I?

   _____

4. I'm a doctor. I move the spine. I correct nervous disorders that way. Who am I?

   _____

5. My patients have trouble hearing and speaking normally. I plan therapy programs to help them communicate more effectively. Who am I?

   _____

6. I teach music to help my patients express their feelings and do something that makes them feel better about themselves. I work with patients in such places as rehabilitation centers and mental hospitals. Who am I?

   _____

7. I'm a doctor. I treat patients with bone, muscle, or nerve disorders. Depending on the problem, I perform surgery or prescribe drugs. Who am I?

   _____

8. I help physical therapists such as Julie treat physically disabled patients. I often get patients ready for treatment and help them do exercises. Who am I?

   _____

Exploring Careers—Instructor's Guide ©1990, JIST Works, Inc., Indianapolis, Indiana

PHYSICAL THERAPIST

9. I'm a doctor. I perform operations to correct bone problems. Who am I?

   _____

10. I plan and direct activities such as sports, arts and crafts, and social functions for patients in hospitals and other institutions. Who am I?

    _____

11. I teach dance to help my patients express their feelings and do something that makes them feel better about themselves. I work with patients in such places as rehabilitation centers and mental hospitals. Who am I?

    _____

12. I help occupational therapists treat patients who are mentally or physically disabled. I might teach patients to dress themselves, to play games, to enjoy dramatics, or to make ceramics. Who am I?

    _____

13. I operate equipment that helps patients breathe. Who am I?

    _____

MUSEUM CURATOR

A. Volunteer to work in a museum during the summer or after school. Talk to the curators about their work. Get a feel for the museum environment.

B. Visit a museum in your community. Arrange for a guided tour. Observe the way in which exhibits, publications, and such educational programs as lectures, films, and workshops all carry out the focus of the museum—art, natural history, science and industry, or another subject.

C. Join a local archaeological or historical society. Find out if there are organizations in your community actively concerned with historic preservation.

D. Invite a curator, art conservator, or other museum worker to speaker to your class. Ask the speaker to talk about job duties, training, and the rewards and frustrations of the work. Arrange for a demonstration of historic preservation techniques if possible.

E. Ask your teacher to arrange a class tour of a historic landmark in your state. There are historic landmarks throughout the country: Colonial communities in the East, plantations in the South, the French sector in New Orleans, Spanish missions in the Southwest, Indian and pioneer settlements in the West. In addition, almost all state capitals have buildings of historical importance, as do many older college campuses. Contact your state historical society, state travel commission, or local chamber of commerce for more information about historic landmarks near you.

F. Use school assignments and activities to strengthen your knowledge of history and its relevance to our lives. Join the history club in your school. Take as many history courses as possible. Ask your history teachers to suggest research projects. Read about historical topics that interest you.

G. Use a historical subject or issue as the basis for a project in a social studies or English class.
  - Do research on a historic building in your area. Find out when it was built and determine what uses it's been put to since then. For help with your research, try the public library, your local historical society, or the planning department of your local government.
  - Prepare a report on the history, folklore, culture, and current situation of an American Indiana tribe. If you were arranging a museum exhibit about this tribe, what items would you include?
  - Make a poster that shows the place of origin and period of arrival of immigrants to the United States. Choose one country and show how some of the ideas, customs, and names of people from that country have become part of American life.

H. Explore your genealogy. To get started, ask the assistance of your parents and relatives. Begin by interviewing your parents, grandparents, and other members of your family. Later on, you'll want to track down certificates of births, deaths, and marriages, and deeds, wills, and records of real estate transactions. Your history teacher and local historical society can offer suggestions on where to start looking for records such as these.

I. Join the staff of your school newspaper. Writing is an important skill for museum curators.

J. Collect and mount at least one coin for every year as far back as possible.

K. Collect and mount stamps from various countries. Show how to use stamp catalogs. Demonstrate how to use a perforation gauge to figure perforation measurements, a watermark detector to identify stamps, a magnifying glass to study their design and condition, and tongs and hinges to mount stamps in an album.

Exploring Careers—Instructor's Guide ©1990, JIST Works, Inc., Indianapolis, Indiana

MUSEUM CURATOR

L. If you are a Girl Scout, see if your local troop has the From Dreams to Reality program for exploring careers. Troops may also offer opportunities to test career interests through internships, service aide and community action projects, and proficiency badges in a number of areas including Stamp Collecting, World Heritage, and My Country.

M. If you are a Boy Scout, try for merit badges in Genealogy, Coin Collecting, and Stamp Collecting.

N. Write for information on museum careers to the American Association of Museums, 1055 Thomas Jefferson Street, N.W., Washington, D.C. 20007.

O. Write for information on careers as a historian to the American Historical Association, 400 A Street, S.E., Washington, D.C. 20003, National Trust for Historic Preservation, 1785 Massachusetts Ave., N.W., Washington, D.C. 20036, and American Association for State and Local History, 172 Second Avenue North, Nashville, Tennessee 37201.

MUSEUM CURATOR

ACTIVITY 37

Name _____
Class _____

MUSEUM CURATOR
Related Occupations

Museum curators are not the only workers concerned with history and historic preservation. The functions of other workers in this field are described below. Match these functions with the job titles listed below. Write your answers in the space provided.

> **Art conservator**
> **Conservation technician**
> **Restorer, lace and textiles**
> **Museum technician**
> **Biographer**
> **Archivist**
>
> **Supervisor, historic sites**
> **Paintings restorer**
> **Fine arts packer**
> **Armorer technician**
> **Genealogist**
> **Archaeologist**

1. I write about the careers or lives of famous people. I get information from diaries, news accounts, personal correspondence, relatives, and business associates of my subjects. Who am I?

   _____

2. I evaluate, classify, and maintain historically valuable materials including government records, letters from famous persons, charters of organizations, maps, motion pictures, and still pictures. I write descriptions of materials so that people will know what is available and how best to make use of it. Who am I?

   _____

3. I prepare items for museum collections and exhibits. I use electric drills, chisels, plaster, glue, and many other tools and materials. Who am I?

   _____

4. I clean, reweave, and mount ancient textile and lace materials for display in textile museums. Who am I?

   _____

5. I repair and clean art objects such as pottery, etchings, and tapestries to restore them to their natural appearance. Who am I?

   _____

6. I try to identify the ancestors of a family or individual. I consult many kinds of documents including records or birth, deaths, and marriages. Who am I?

   _____

7. I try to reconstruct the history and customs of cultures that no longer exist. I study the remains of homes, clothing, and other evidences of human life recovered by excavation. Who am I?

   _____

Exploring Careers—Instructor's Guide ©1990, JIST Works, Inc., Indianapolis, Indiana

MUSEUM CURATOR

8. I supervise workers who repair and conserve art objects. I examine art objects using X-rays and special lights to determine their authenticity, need for repair, and the best method of preservation. Who am I?

   _____

9. I restore and prepare exhibits of medieval arms and armor such as helmets, guns, and swords. Who am I?

   _____

10. I clean, retouch, and remount damaged and faded paintings. Who am I?

    _____

11. I direct the activities of people involved in investigating and preserving historic homes, battlefields, and other landmarks. We prepare brochures, exhibits, maps, and photographs to encourage people to visit historic sites. Who am I?

    _____

12. I determine the best way to pack, transport, and store valuable historic items to minimize damage and deterioration. Who am I?

    _____

POLITICIAN

A. Watch our government in action. Visit the Congress or your State legislature. Attend a legislative session in your county or municipality.

B. Study the issues and attend public meetings of local government bodies such as the council of governments, city or county council, or board of education. Ask questions. Discuss the proceedings with your family and friends.

C. Invite an elected official or a member of his or her staff to speak to your class. Ask the speaker to discuss his or her job, background, and plans for the future. What does the speaker like and dislike about a career in politics?

D. Take an active interest in student government. Run for office. Manage the campaign of one of your classmates. Write an article on the campaign for your school or local newspaper.

E. Volunteer in a local political campaign. You might stuff envelopes, deliver campaign literature, put up posters, answer the telephone, or go from door to door urging people to vote for your candidate.

F. Some communities have a Youth Council whose function is to speak on the behalf of young people and promote youth activities. Call the mayor's office to find out whether there is such a group in your community.

G. Follow the campaign of a candidate for political office. Clip newspaper and magazine articles and save brochures and flyers. Prepare a notebook or bulletin board that shows the ups and downs of the campaign and the final outcome.

H. Plan and conduct a survey on an important issue in your school. You might survey both teachers and students so that there will be two groups to compare. Developing the questionnaire, distributing it, and tabulating and analyzing the responses will introduce you to the survey method of doing social science research.

I. Use voting procedures as a topic for a report in your social studies or English class. Learn the qualifications for voting. Find out the dates for registration and for voting in the primaries and the general election. Where are the polling places in your community? What do pollwatchers do? Who counts the ballots? Your local board of elections, or a civic group such as Common Cause or the League of Women Voters, can help you with your research.

J. As a project for a social studies class, prepare a chart of the organization of your village, town, city, or county government.

K. Develop communications skills by writing for your school newspaper, joining the debate team or speech club, or writing poetry and short stories.

L. Join a Government and Politics, Journalism, or Youth Leadership Explorer Post if there is one in your area. Exploring is open to young men and women aged 14 through 20. To find out about Explorer posts in your area, call "Boy Scouts of America" listed in your phone book, and ask for the "Exploring Division."

M. If you are a Boy Scout, earn a merit badge in Citizenship in the Community, Nation, and World.

N. If you are a Girl Scout, see if your local troop has the From Dreams to Reality program for exploring careers. Troops may also offer opportunities to test career interests through internships, service aide and community action projects, and proficiency badges in a number of areas including My Country, My Government, and Reporter.

O. Write for information on careers in political science to the American Political Science Association, 1527 New Hampshire Avenue, N.W., Washington, D.C. 20036.

MINISTER

A. Volunteer your services to your church or synagogue. As you find out how many opportunities there are to help, you will get a better idea of the varied activities in which members of the clergy are involved. Volunteers assist in music programs as instrumentalists, singers, composers, arrangers, and directors. They type, file, answer the telephone, stuff envelopes, and handle other clerical duties in the office. They put out the newsletter or weekly bulletin, write press releases, and handle publicity. They help with fundraising drives. Volunteers staff social action programs including hotlines, Meals on Wheels, and aid to disaster victims. Youth programs, religious education programs, day care centers, and vacation Bible schools also use volunteers.

B. Volunteer to work with children as a tutor or aide in an elementary school. Help out at a nursery school or Head Start program. Offer to help direct children in arts and crafts, music, or sports at a summer recreation program. This will help you develop leadership and teaching skills and test your ability to handle a group.

C. Volunteer to work in a program that will bring you into close contact with a wider variety of people than you normally meet at your school, church, or synagogue. This will broaden your knowledge of community needs and increase your understanding of human behavior.

D. Collect magazines, clothing, and funds for a missionary drive.

E. Take part in your church or synagogue visitation campaign to encourage people to attend religious services.

F. Run for youth deacon.

G. Set a goal for reading the Bible from cover to cover.

H. Compete in a local Bible drill.

I. Try out for your school debate team. Public speaking is an essential part of the clergy's job.

J. Join or organize a prayer or study group. Test your organizational skills and your ability to work effectively within a group.

K. Put yourself in the helper role on a daily basis. This may involve listening to a friend talk through a problem, visiting elderly people in the community who are confined to home, or becoming a big brother or big sister to a disadvantaged or handicapped child.

L. Read books and magazines on religious occupations. Talk with your priest, minister, or rabbi about what it's like to have a religious occupation. Test your interest.

M. For more information about careers in this field, write to the Interdenominational National Council of Churches of Christ, Unit of Professional Church Leadership, 475 Riverside Drive, New York, NY 10027; Catholic National Conference of Diocesan Vocation Directors, 1307 S. Wabash, Suite 350, Chicago, IL 60605; or the B'nai B'rith Career and Counseling Service, 1640 Rhode Island Avenue, N.W., Washington, D.C. 20036.

MINISTER

ACTIVITY 38

Name _____
Class _____

MINISTER
Related Occupations

Helping people with their personal problems is an important part of a minister's job. The desire to help others is just as important for members of the clergy in other religious faiths. Workers in other "helping" occupations spend much of their time advising and counseling people, too.

Eight occupations are listed below. See if you can match each job title with the correct description. Write your answers in the space provided.

Psychologist	**Christian Science Practitioner**
Chaplain	**Rabbi**
Missionary	**Social Worker**
School Counselor	**Priest**

1. I am the spiritual head of a Jewish congregation. I teach and interpret Jewish law and tradition.

   _____

2. I give religious counsel and leadership in the Armed Forces, police departments, prisons, colleges and universities, hospitals, and other places.

   _____

3. I help individuals and groups cope with problems that, at times, are overwhelming: Poverty, illness, unemployment, family disputes, antisocial behavior, and inadequate housing.

   _____

4. I am the spiritual head of a Catholic congregation.

   _____

5. I carry a religious message to people who are not of my faith.

   _____

6. I help students select courses, explore career possibilities, and decide what to do after they graduate. I collect and analyze information that tells me something about students' interests, aptitudes, abilities, and personality characteristics. Most of this information comes from records, tests, and interviews. I collect occupational and educational information, and encourage students to browse through it.

   _____

7. I practice spiritual healing through prayer alone in accordance with the teaching of my religion.

   _____

8. I study people and try to understand why individuals and groups behave as they do. My research is put to use in many fields: Mental health, juvenile delinquency, drug abuse, crowd control, early childhood education, and counseling of retirees, for example.

   _____

SOCIAL WORKER

A. Volunteer to work in a social service agency in your community. There are more agencies than you might think. Try, for example, the local department of public welfare, a family service agency, agencies run by Catholic, Protestant, and Jewish organizations, or the Salvation Army. Volunteers answer telephones, greet and direct visitors, provide clerical assistance, and sort donations. They may also visit the lonely and work with children.

B. Volunteer to work in a crisis counseling center. This is a good place to learn about the most critical problems in your area and to find out how community organizations are handling them. Volunteers may greet visitors, do clerical work, and solicit or help distribute donations of food, clothing, fuel, and other necessities for the center's clients.

C. Develop a one-to-one relationship with a youngster who has had few positive influences in his or her life. The Big Brother and Big Sister programs offer opportunities of this kind. So do welfare and probation departments, YMCAs and YWCAs, Boys' Clubs, Girls' Clubs, and family service programs run by Catholic, Protestant, and Jewish organizations.

D. Involve yourself in the activities of a neighborhood or community center. You can develop organizational and leadership skills by helping direct children in sports, arts and crafts, music, or drama. You might tutor children or adults. Or you might work in fund raising and publicity for the center's programs. All of these activities will give you experience organizing social service programs and working with people.

E. Invite a social worker to speak to your class about his or her job. Ask the speaker to explain what he or she does and to mention the rewards and frustrations of the work. Prepare questions ahead of time.

F. Look for opportunities to work with people of different ages and backgrounds.
- Volunteer to help with younger children at a day camp or summer recreation program.
- Spend time with handicapped or retarded children. Girls' Clubs, Boys' Clubs, Red Cross, Scout troops, Campfire Girls, and other youth organizations offer such opportunities.
- Volunteer to entertain or visit residents in a nursing home.

G. If you are a Boy Scout, try for a merit badge in Family Living. Test your interest in working with and learning about your family and others.

H. If you are a Girl Scout, try for proficiency badges in child care. Caring for children may test your interest in a career that requires concerned interaction with others. Also, see if your local troop has the From Dreams to Reality program of career exploration. Troops also sponsor service aid and community action projects.

I. Join a Child Care, Communication, or Social Work Explorer Post if there is one in your area. Exploring is open to young men and women aged 14 through 20. To find out about Explorer posts in your area, call "Boy Scouts of America" listed in your phone book, and ask for the "Exploring Division."

J. For information about career and education opportunities in the field of social work, write to the National Association of Social Workers, 1425 H Street, N.W., Suite 600, Washington, D.C. 20005, and to the Council on Social Work Education, 345 East 46th street, New York, NY 10017.

SOCIAL WORKER

ACTIVITY 39

Name _____
Class _____

SOCIAL WORKER
Related Occupations

Social workers aren't the only people who help individuals and groups with problems. Eight jobs are described below. Unscramble the letters to discover who these workers are.

Caseworker	Community Organization Worker
Minister	Parole Officer
Probation Officer	Recreation Leader
School Counselor	Social Welfare Administrator

1. **OPLRAE CREFIFO.** I work with law offenders when they get out of jail. I advise them about completing school or getting job training and help them look for a job and a place to live. I try to learn enough about them and their backgrounds to have some real influence; my goal is to help them find a way of making an honest living.

   _____

2. **CTAIERERNO RLADEE.** I organize recreational activities such as arts and crafts, sports, games, music, dramatics, camping and hobbies. I work with groups of people in camps, community centers, YMCAs and YWCAs, senior centers, and other places.

   _____

3. **REWKERCSAO.** I help individuals and families who need the assistance of a social service agency. I interview clients with problems ranging from runaway children to illness, no money, and eviction. I listen first. Then I try to help my clients work out a solution. Often I put them in touch with other agencies that can help, too.

   _____

4. **STRENIMI.** I provide spiritual leadership within my community.

   _____

5. **BAOPRONIT CREFIFO.** I work with law offenders while they are on probation. Sometimes I decide which juvenile cases belong in the courts and which should be handled by a social service agency.

   _____

6. **CHSOLO SEROLUNOC.** I help students deal with things that bother them—personal problems, family problems, failing grades. I also help them plan courses and school activities that best fit their interests and abilities.

   _____

Exploring Careers—Instructor's Guide ©1990, JIST Works, Inc., Indianapolis, Indiana

SOCIAL WORKER

7. NITYUMOMC NATIGROONIZA WKEROR. I work with community groups and advise them on the kinds of action that will meet their interests and needs. I work with all kinds of groups: Senior citizens afraid of crime, tenants facing a rent increase, street gangs, children with no place to play, parents trying to organize a day care center. I help the group organize, raise funds, and take action.

8. CILOAS FAREWEL MINIADTRATORIS. I run a social service agency. As an administrator, it's up to me to see that the agency's programs meet our clients' needs—that people in real trouble don't run into a lot of red tape, for one thing. Selecting, training, and supervising the staff are important parts of the job. Representing my agency to community groups and citizens is also important and I frequently go to meetings and make speeches.

ARCHITECT

A. Ask your teacher to arrange an architectural tour of a historic landmark in your state. There are historic landmarks in every state: Colonial communities in the East, plantations in the South, the French sector in New Orleans, Spanish mission in the Southwest, Indian and pioneer settlements in the West. In addition, almost all state capitals have buildings of historical importance, as do many older college campuses. Contact your state Historical Society, State Travel Commission, or local Chamber of Commerce for more information about historic landmarks near you.

B. As a project for a social studies or art class, conduct an architectural tour of a distinctive neighborhood in your community. The area you select for your tour might be the neighborhood where you live or go to school; a historic section; a riverfront or lakefront area; or the newest part of your community.

C. Identify several buildings in the area you select. Write one paragraph about each of these buildings, giving the street address, approximate year of construction, and interesting historical and/or architectural details. For help with your research, try the public library, a historical society, the planning department of your local government, and local architects. Prepare a drawing that includes the major buildings in your tour.

D. As a project for a social studies or art class, choose an interesting building in your community. Learn its history. When was it built? Have there been any additions or changes since it was built? Draw exterior views of the building. Construct a small cardboard model of it.

E. As a project for an art class, design your "dream house" or design a large project such as an airport or shopping center.

F. Ask your teacher to arrange a class visit to a construction site.

G. Design and build a doghouse, birdhouse, or playhouse.

H. Invite an architect to speak to your class about his or her job. Ask the speaker to bring some plans or drawings and explain them to the class.

I. Take the dimensions of your classroom as a project for a mathematics class. Then draw the room to scale, letting 1/2 inch equal 1 foot. Include all permanent objects in your plan, including windows, doors, and radiators. Translate the measurements into metric units.

J. As a project for an art class, prepare a landscape design. Show the location of the lawn, bushes and shrubs, walkways, trees, flower gardens, rock gardens, ponds, benches, gazebos, and any other features you decide to include.

K. Invite a local building inspector to class to explain what inspectors look for when inspecting new residential buildings for approval of construction. Ask the speaker to bring copies of any forms he or she uses on the job.

L. Invent a new kind of structure as a project for an art or mathematics class. You might use unusual concepts such as domes, treehouses, or tents. You might use unusual shapes such as pyramids, cones, or spheres. Or you might use unusual materials such as plastic, thatch, or cardboard.

M. Join an Architecture Explorer Post, if there is one in your area. Exploring is open to young men and women aged 14 through 20. To find out about Explorer posts in your area, call "Boy Scouts of America" listed in your phone book, and ask for the "Exploring Division."

N. If you are a Boy Scout, try for Drafting, Landscape Architecture, Surveying, and Model Design and Building merit badges.

O. If you are a Girl Scout, see if your local troop has the From Dreams to Reality program for exploring careers. Troops may also offer opportunities to try out careers through internships and service aide and community action projects.

ARCHITECT

P. As a project for a science fair, design an environment for non-humans. You might want to design a "habitat" for animals in a zoo, or something as fantastic as a shopping mall for beings from Venus. If you decide to design something for beings from another planet, remember to describe them first. For example, the Venusian shopper might breathe water, see through a hole in the top of his or her head, or move by bouncing off walls.

Q. Write for career information to the American Institute of Architects, 1735 New York Avenue, N.W., Washington, D.C. 20006.

ARCHITECT

ACTIVITY 40

Name _____
Class _____

ARCHITECT
Related Occupations

Architects aren't the only people whose jobs involve planning, designing, and building objects or structures. Match the occupational title with the correct definition. Write your answers in the space provided.

Building contractor **Industrial designer**
Civil engineer **Landscape architect**
Planner **Drafter**
Interior design **Surveyor**

1. Plans lawns and gardens for parks, airports, hospitals, schools, stores, factories, and homes. May plan and arrange trees, shrubbery, open spaces, and other features, as well as supervise any grading, construction, and planting.

   _____

2. Contracts to perform construction work by an estimate of of the cost of the work, submitting a bid, and having it accepted. Purchases materials and hires labor for construction, and supervises the work.

   _____

3. Prepares detailed drawings based on rough sketches, specifications, and calculations made by scientists, engineers, architects, and designers. Also calculates the strength, quality, quantity, and cost of materials.

   _____

4. Helps communities make decisions to solve their social, economic, and environmental problems. Develops programs to provide for future development of urban, suburban, or rural communities.

   _____

5. Measures construction sites, helps establish official land boundaries, assists in setting land valuations, and collects information for maps and charts.

   _____

6. Plans and supervises the design, color scheme, and arrangement of building interiors and furnishings. Estimates costs and selects materials to present to client for approval.

   _____

7. Designs and supervises the construction of roads, harbors, airports, tunnels, bridges, water supply and sewage systems, and buildings.

   _____

8. Combines artistic talent with knowledge of marketing, materials, and methods of production to improve the appearance and functional design of a product.

   _____

ARCHITECT

ACTIVITY 41

Name _____

Class _____

ARCHITECT
Math

Architects use mathematics in their jobs every day. Try your hand at the following simple examples of ways in which an architect uses mathematics. Write your answers in the space provided.

1. An architect is planning a house for a couple who does not want to spend more than $70,000. Building costs in the area are $35 per square foot. What is the largest house (in square feet) that the couple can afford?

   _____

2. An architect has been commissioned to renovate an old house. The owners do not want to spend over $50,000 on the entire job, including the cost of the house, which was $22,500. The architect already has contracted out plumbing work of $3,000, electrical work of $3,500, and heating and air-conditioning work of $6,000. How much money is left for completing the job?

   _____

3. An architect must design a rectangular shed of exactly 200 square feet. Give the dimension of at least three different rectangles that will fulfill the requirements.

   a. _____

   b. _____

   c. _____

NEWSPAPER REPORTER

A. Join the staff of your school newspaper or yearbook.

B. Volunteer to help with the newsgathering, editing, and production of the newsletter for your synagogue, church, or community organization.

C. Contact the editor of your local newspaper and offer to cover sports activities at your school.

D. Arrange to submit a regular column about activities at your school to your local newspaper or radio station.

E. Volunteer to handle publicity for a school event such as a science fair, concert, career day, or awards ceremony. Prepare a press release; arrange for a radio interview.

F. Design a new kind of magazine. First decide who your audience will be, and what kinds of news and features you will include. Make your magazine different in some way from other magazines. Design the cover and the layout.

G. Join a writing or journalism club such as Future Journalists of America or the Quill and Scroll Society.

H. Creative writing is important in all journalistic endeavors. Try developing this skill through one or more of the following types of creative expression:
  - Start a creative writing magazine if your school doesn't have one.
  - Enter a poetry reading contest.
  - Ask permission to do poetry readings over the loudspeaker before the morning announcements. You might want to read old favorites or compose your own.
  - Write new words to old songs.
  - Write poetry, short stories, or essays in your spare time. Ask your English teacher for comments on your work.

I. Write a letter to the editor of your local newspaper about an important issue in your community. See if your letter is printed.

J. Invite a freelance writer to speak to your English class about his or her work. Prepare questions in advance on story ideas, publication possibilities, and the pros and cons of freelance writing.

K. Invite the editor of a weekly newspaper and the editor of a daily newspaper to class to discuss their jobs. Explain in advance that your class is interested in learning some of the similarities and differences in their jobs.

L. Join a debate team or club.

M. Use one or more of the following topics for discussion in your English or social studies class:
  - A reporter for a national newspaper must decide whether to write an article that exposes a friend's wrongdoing.
  - A reporter for a small suburban newspaper is asked not to write an important piece because the publisher knows it will offend a prominent client.
  - An editor wants a novelist to add a chapter with some violent action so that the book will sell better even though the addition will detract from the theme of the novel.
  - Where should one draw the line between a newspaper's right to know facts versus an individual's or company's right to privacy?

N. If you are a Girl Scout, see if your local troop has the From Dreams to Reality program for exploring careers. Troops may also offer opportunities to test career interests through proficiency badges in a number of areas including Creative Writer, Player, Producer, and Reporter.

O. If you are a Boy Scout, try for Communications, Journalism, Public Speaking, or Reading merit badges.

NEWSPAPER REPORTER

P. Join a Journalism or Communications Explorer Post, if there is one in your area. Exploring is open to young men and women aged 14 through 20. To find out about Explorer posts in your area, call "Boy Scouts of America" listed in your phone book, and ask for the "Exploring Division."

Q. Write for career information to The Newspaper Fund, Inc., P.O. Box 300, Princeton, NJ 08543; Society of Professional Journalists (Sigma Delta Chi), 53 W. Jackson Blvd., Suite 731, Chicago, IL 60604; and American Newspaper Publishers, Association Foundation, P.O. Box 17407, Dulles International Airport, Washington, D.C. 20041.

NEWSPAPER REPORTER

ACTIVITY 42-1

Name _____
Class _____

NEWSPAPER REPORTER
Related Occupations

Newspaper reporters aren't the only people with writing and publishing jobs. The crossword puzzle below includes quite a few writing occupations—and some newspaper "lingo" as well. You will find the clues on the next page.

NEWSPAPER REPORTER

ACTIVITY 42-2

NEWSPAPER REPORTER
Crossword Puzzle Clues

Down

1. One who writes verse.

2. A(n) _____ writer creates stories about imaginary characters.

3. Artist who prepares advertising or other newspaper or magazine page layout for reproduction. (2 words)

5. A person who is responsible for setting the policy of a newspaper or other periodical and deciding what will be printed.

6. Someone who writes short stories. (3 words)

8. A person who writes only the words to a song writes the _____.

11. A general term for a person who writes inventive poetry, short stories, or drama. (2 words)

12. Writes material for pamphlets or brochures. (2 words)

13. Someone who writes the messages on birthday, anniversary, and other holiday cards. (3 words)

15. A person who markets clients' manuscripts to editors and publishers. (2 words)

16. This person tells a story using photographs instead of words.

18. Someone who teaches journalism. (2 words)

20. A person who writes textbooks. (2 words)

21. A newspaper writer who reviews and comments on the fine arts, such as painting, sculpture, and architecture. (3 words)

24. A newspaper staff person (often an editor) who writes an article expressing an opinion. (2 words)

27. One of the questions that should be answered by a reporter in his or her opening paragraph.

30. A(n) _____ reporter is a first-rate or expert reporter.

32. Speech writers produce *written* speeches while public speakers give _____ speeches.

34. It helps for a newspaper reporter to be a good _____ since he or she will probably spend a lot of time composing or rewriting at the typewriter.

35. A line printed above a newspaper or magazine article, telling who wrote it.

36. Another question that should be answered by a reporter in his or her opening paragraph.

Across

2. A(n) _____ reporter writes about money matters.

4. One who writes about or comments on newly published books. (2 words)

7. One who writes drama.

9. Another question that should be answered by a reporter in his or her opening paragraph.

10. One who comments on motion pictures.

NEWSPAPER REPORTER

12. Someone who writes an account of another's life.

14. Someone who writes material designed to promote sales. (3 words)

17. Another question that should be answered by a reporter in his or her opening paragraph.

19. A person who writes novels.

22. A news or wire service.

23. One of the questions that should be answered by a reporter in his or her opening paragraph.

24. Abbreviation for "English."

25. A(n) _____ reporter is a novice or beginning reporter.

26. Another question that should be answered by a reporter in his or her opening paragraph.

28. Someone who puts scientific and technical information into language that can readily be understood by others. (2 words)

29. A news or wire service.

31. A person on a newspaper or magazine who selects, arranges, and revises the "copy," or written material, in preparation for publication. (2 words)

33. Someone who writes about athletic events.

37. One who writes essays.

38. A newspaper or magazine reporter who sends in articles from a particular geographical location (as in a foreign "_____").

39. A person who writes the written part of a play or radio show.

Exploring Careers—Instructor's Guide   ©1990, JIST Works, Inc., Indianapolis, Indiana

MUSICIAN

A. If you play an instrument or enjoy singing, get together with some friends and form a musical group. Meet regularly; once a week is probably about right. Play for the fun if it. Offer to perform at a hospital or nursing home.

B. Make a tape recording of your playing or singing. Hearing yourself on tape can help you improve your sound.

C. Join your school band, orchestra, or chorus. Join a community orchestra or chorus. Join a church choir.

D. Participate in school drama or musical productions. Performing can help you develop stage presence.

E. Enter talent shows.

F. Perform in amateur nights, open stages, or even gong shows at local coffee houses or clubs. Many clubs hold these once a month or so. They are a good way to test yourself in front of a real audience, and maybe even get bookings.

G. If you think you're good enough, try to get an engagement to play in a local coffeehouse. The pay may be low, but the exposure will be good.

H. Invite a church organist, school band director, chorus director, music teacher, or other musician in your community to speak to your class about his or her career.

I. Use music as a topic for a report in your English class. Investigate one or more types of music such as classical, folk, jazz, country and western, rhythm and blues, rock and roll, or soul. Discuss the origins and development of the musical style you choose, and give examples of works.

J. Use the biography of a musician for a book report in your English class.

K. Try to set a limerick or poem to music. Take a familiar song and write new words for it.

L. List the different radio stations in your area, noting the different types of music that each specializes in.

M. Check out a record from your local library to learn more about different styles of music.

N. Ask your teacher to invite an audio-engineer or disc jockey from a nearby radio station or recording studio to speak to your class about his or her job.

O. Volunteer to organize musical activities for young children at a Sunday School, nursery school, day care center, or summer camp.

P. As a report for your science class, find out how a computer "writes" music.

Q. Write a musical commercial for an up-coming school event, organize the talent to perform it, and play it over the public address system with the daily announcements.

R. Take charge of coordinating the music for a school dance. This means planning what songs should be played and what order to play them in. You may want to use a tape recorder instead of a recorder player, and tape the songs ahead of time in the order you want them.

S. Not everybody working in the field of music is a performer. Production and sales, for example, are important aspects of the music industry. Invite the owner or manager of a record or music store to speak to your class about his or her business. Prepare questions in advance about running a small music business.

T. Compile a directory of performing music opportunities in your community, include both paid and unpaid opportunities.

U. Invite a piano tuner to visit your class and talk about his or her work. Ask the speaker to talk about training opportunities and job prospects.

MUSICIAN

V. As a report for your science or social studies class, examine the ways in which technological change has affected musicians. For example, you might explore the effect of tape recorders, radio, amplification equipment, electronic instruments (guitars, organs), cartridge players in cars, electronic equipment such as synthesizers, or computerized composition. Consider, as examples, the effect of recordings on the use of live musicians for rehearsals; the effect of the spread of dance clubs on the employment of live musicians; and the effect of amplification on trends in styles of music.

W. If you are a Girl Scout, see if your local troop has the From Dreams to Reality program for exploring careers. Troops may also offer opportunities to test career interests through proficiency badges in a number of areas including Minstrel and Music Maker.

X. If you are a Boy Scout, try for the Music merit badge.

Y. Join a Music Explorer Post, if there is one in your area. Exploring is open to young men and women aged 14 through 20. To find out about Explorer posts in your area, call "Boy Scouts of America" listed in your phone book, and ask for the "Exploring Division."

Z. Write for career information to National Association of Schools of Music, 11250 Roger Bacon Drive, #21, Reston, Virginia 22090; and Music Educators National Conference, 1902 Association Drive, Reston, Virginia 22091.

Exploring Careers—Instructor's Guide   ©1990, JIST Works, Inc., Indianapolis, Indiana

MUSICIAN

ACTIVITY 43

Name _____
Class _____

MUSICIAN
Related Occupations

There are many different jobs in the field of music. The puzzle below includes 23 of them. How many can you find? Words may be backwards or forwards, horizontal, vertical, or diagonal. Circle or shade your answers.

Arranger	**Folk musician**	**Musicologist**	**Pianist**
Chorus director	**Instrumentalist**	**Music teacher**	**Record producer**
Church musician	**Music critic**	**Music theater director**	**Rock musician**
Composer	**Vocalist**	**Music therapist**	**Studio musician**
Conductor	**Orchestrator**	**Opera singer**	**Instrument salesperson**
Disc jockey	**Music librarian**	**Instrument craftsperson**	

```
I T B L A N O R C H E S T R A T O R O C T I
S N A I R A R B I L C I S U M C P B A M L N
U S S O D T C H U R C H M U S I C I A N A S
I N S T R U M E N T A L I S T H M A R I M T
R A K S R J E F O L R C I A N U P L T U S R
M I D L M U S I C O L O G I S T A N S F E U
I C L O U O M A V O C A L I S T T I O N I M
S I M R A Y A E S M A N C A R O C I P E T E
T S Y O D P I A N I S T S E N C H B E V E N
N U L T R A N S O T E L S O R V I A R N N T
O M S C U E S T R A S O U I L I B A A A G C
U K T U Y B T I C F P A T G R R A R S I A R
G L A D E V O H O M N I L S A C H R I C O A
H O B N K S E G O A C R I E M O T A N I T F
S F O O C R W C U F T E N T S R I N G S S T
A R E C O R D P R O D U C E R P N G E U N S
X S L A J H O U S T A V I R S T E E R M R P
M U S I C T H E R A P I S T A O P R L K P E
J O H P S T U D I O M U S I C I A N S C T R
O M U S I C T H E A T E R D I R E C T O R S
R O S I D G U A V I S E N T U P T P I R N O
E D P R U R O T C E R I D S U R O H C P A N
```

FARMER

A. Listen to the farmer on your local radio or television station. Look up any terms whose meaning you don't know.

B. Your newspaper's financial section lists the day's prices for a variety of farm products. Follow the price of a particular product, such as wheat or corn, over a period of time. Can you see how fluctuations in crop prices would affect you as a farmer?

C. Write a report on one or more of the following things that farmers must deal with: Plant varieties, plant diseases, cattle varieties, animal diseases, insects, chemicals, fertilizers, and soil types.

D. Go to a livestock auction if there is one in your area. Make a list of the grades and types of animals sold at the auction and the prices they sell for.

E. Visit the meat counter of your local grocery store or supermarket. Note the various cuts and grades of beef that are sold. Can you see any difference in the various grades of meat?

F. Visit a farm equipment dealer if there is one in your area. Find out why there is such a wide range in tractor sizes and horsepower. Look at the various farm implements that are for sale and try to figure out how they work, and what they are used for.

G. Try to get permission to accompany a veterinarian who treats farm animals. Note the types of animals that are treated, what some of the most common ailments are, and how the veterinarian handles these ailments.

H. For more information on farming as a career, read *Careers in Agriculture and Natural Resources*, published in 1976 by the National Association of State Universities and Land Grant Colleges. Your library or State agricultural college may have this booklet.

I. Join a farming organization for young people such as the Future Farmers of America or the 4-H Club. Members of these organizations gain practical experience in agriculture and take part in fairs, agricultural contests, horse shows, and many other activities.

J. If you are a Boy Scout, try for merit badges in Agriculture, Animal Science, Beekeeping, Botany, Farm Arrangement, Farm Mechanics, Farm Records, Gardening, Plant Science, Rabbit Raising, Soil and Water Conservation and Veterinary Science.

K. If you are a Girl Scout, see if your local troop has the From Dreams to Reality program of career exploration. Troops may also offer opportunities to try out careers through internships, service aide and community action projects, and proficiency badges in a number of areas including Animal Kingdom, Conservation, Food Raiser, Horsewoman, and Plant Kingdom.

L. Plan a small garden for your yard or any small plot of land you can get permission to use. Here are some things you might want to do before you plant anything.

- Obtain soil samples from the plot you have selected and take them to your county agent for testing. When the results come back, ask the agent to explain them to you and to recommend what to plant and what kind of fertilizer to use.

- Send for some garden seed catalogs. These will give you an idea of the wide number of crop varieties available and provide valuable information on planning your garden.

M. Try to obtain first-hand experience in farming by getting a part-time or summer job on a farm or ranch.

FARMER

N. Join an Agriculture, Veterinary, or Conservation/Ecology Explorer Post if there is one in your area. Exploring is open to young men and women aged 14 through 20. To find out about Explorer posts in your area, call "Boy Scouts of America" listed in your phone book, and ask for the "Exploring Division."

O. Write the Dean of Agriculture of your State's land grant college or university. The Dean can provide you with information on careers in agriculture, and the training they require.

FARMER

ACTIVITY 44 Name _____
 Class _____

FARMER
Related Occupations

Farmers aren't the only people involved in producing agricultural products. People in many other occupations work outdoors and assist in the production of crops and animals. Some of these jobs are described below. If you need to, refer to the list of job titles. Write your answers in the space provided.

Agricultural pilot **Agricultural products broker**
Farm equipment mechanic **Farm laborer**
Farm manager **Veterinarian**

1. Although I don't own a farm, I have the same planning and management responsibilities that a farmer has. Who am I?

   _____

2. I repair and maintain farm machinery and equipment. I work for a tractor dealer. Who am I?

   _____

3. I do much of the physical labor on the large farm on which I work. Who am I?

   _____

4. I apply fertilizers and insecticides to crops by flying over them with my plane. Who am I?

   _____

5. I act as an agent between farmers and the people who buy their crops. Who am I?

   _____

6. When farmers' animals get sick or need treatment, I am the one who usually diagnoses the problem and treats it. Who am I?

   _____

FARMER

ACTIVITY 45

Name _____

Class _____

FARMER
Math

See if you can solve the following math problems which are typical of some of the simpler calculations farmers must make in planning their activities.

1. Bill Jenkins, a Kansas farmer, plans to raise 600 acres of wheat this year. If Bill gets 40 bushels of wheat per acre, how many bushels will he raise?

   _____

2. Bill plans to spend about $100 per acre on growing the wheat.
   a. At what market price per bushel will Bill break even?

   _____

   b. What price per bushel does he need to get in order to make $24,000?

   _____

3. A farmer plans to put a four-strand barbed wire fence around a 640-acre plot of land (640 acres = 1 section = 1 mile). Barbed wire costs $35 for a 1/4-mile roll. How much will the wire for the fence cost?

   _____

4. A cattle feedlot operator has determined that her cattle gain 1 pound of weight for every five pounds of feed. The price of cattle is now $.50 per pound. Grain costs $4.80 for a 60-pound bushel. What is the operator's profit or loss for each bushel fed?

   _____

COOPERATIVE EXTENSION SERVICE WORKER

A. Plan a small garden for your yard or any small plot of land you can get permission to use. Here are some things you can get permission to use. Here are some things you might want to do before you plant anything.

- Obtain soil samples from the plots you have selected and take them to your county agent for testing. When the results come back, ask the agent to explain them to you and recommend what to plant and what kind of fertilizer to use.
- Send for some garden seed catalogs. These will give you an idea of the wide number of crop varieties available and provide valuable information on planning your garden.

B. Try to obtain first-hand experience in farming by getting a part-time or summer job on a farm or ranch.

C. Write articles for your school newspaper. If your school doesn't have a newsletter, start one. This will help develop your writing skills, which are essential in extension service work.

D. Spend time on hobbies and other activities in which you build, repair, or maintain things. Work on your bicycle. Do carpentry. Check the oil, water, and tires on your family's car. Make repairs around your home. Try an electronics project for your school's science fair. These activities will help you understand the problems that farmers face daily in repairing and maintaining the many buildings and the variety of equipment found on modern farms.

E. Invite your county extension agent to speak to your class about his or her job. Prepare questions in advance.

F. Help teach youngsters about the outdoors. You might lead nature walks and help them learn about the environment by identifying trees, plants, flowers, insects, birds, and other wildlife. This will help you develop teaching and leadership skills.

G. Join a farming organization for young people such as the Future Farmers of America or the 4-H Club. Members of these organizations gain practical experience in agriculture and take part in fairs, agriculture contests, horse shows, and many other activities.

H. Visit the agricultural exhibits at a county or state fair. Usually, there will be young people at the fair exhibiting their own animals. Speak with these young exhibitors and ask them about their animals, what is involved in caring for the animals, and what the exhibitors feel about a career in agriculture.

I. Do a report on the six major breeds of dairy cattle. To help remember what you learned, try to identify the breeds you see on farms whenever you are driving through rural areas.

J. See if you can get permission to visit a farm in your area. While you are there, ask the farmer or farm workers about the products they raise and the different tasks involved with raising these products.

K. If you are a Girl Scout, see if your local troop has the From Dreams to Reality program of career exploration. Troops may also offer opportunities to try out careers through internships, service aide and community action projects, and proficiency badges in a number of areas including Animal Kingdom, Plant Kingdom, Science, Conservation, Games Leader, and Reporter.

L. If you are a Boy Scout, try for merit badges in Agriculture, Animal Science, Beekeeping, Botany, Communications, Environmental Science, Farm Arrangement, Farm Mechanics, Farm Records, Gardening, Pigeon Raising, Plant Science, Public Speaking, Rabbit Raising, Soil and Water Conservation, and Veterinary Science.

COOPERATIVE EXTENSION SERVICE WORKER

M. Join an Agriculture, Conservation/Ecology, Education/Teaching, Veterinary, or Science Explorer Post if there is one in your area. Exploring is open to young men and women aged 14 through 20. To find out about Explorer posts in your area, call "Boy Scouts of America" listed in your phone book, and ask for the "Explorer Division."

N. For more information on a career in agriculture, read *Careers in Agriculture and Natural Resources*, published in 1976 by the National Association of State Universities and Land Grant Colleges. Your state agricultural college can also provide information on crop and animal farming and extension programs in your state.

O. Write to the Science and Education Administration-Extension, U.S. Department of Agriculture, Washington, D.C. 20250, and ask for the pamphlet, *Your Career as an Extension Agent*.

COOPERATIVE EXTENSION SERVICE WORKER

ACTIVITY 46

Name _____

Class _____

COOPERATIVE EXTENSION SERVICE WORKER
Related Occupations

There are many other occupations concerned with improving the productivity of agriculture. Some of these are listed below, along with possible definitions of what the worker does. For each occupation, see if you can choose the correct definition. Circle the correct answer.

1. **Soil Conservationist.**
   a. Provides technical assistance to farmers and others concerned with preventing damage to land or streams.
   b. Makes plastic tarps to prevent soil from becoming bruised during hailstorms.
   c. Evaluates timber stands to determine amount of wildlife they can support.

2. **Veterinarian.**
   a. Administers programs for soldiers leaving the Armed Forces.
   b. Diagnoses, treats, and controls diseases and injuries among animals.
   c. Provides counseling services to aging athletes.

3. **Soil Scientist.**
   a. Categorizes soils according to a national classification system.
   b. Studies effectiveness of various detergents in removing soils.
   c. Encourages the removal of vegetation to help prevent erosion.

4. **Farm Manager.**
   a. Directs the activities of all farmers in a state.
   b. Manages the Federal Agricultural Resource Marketing (FARM) Program.
   c. Plans and directs agricultural activities on large farms.

5. **Animal Breeder.**
   a. Artificially impregnates cows and ewes.
   b. Develops improved breeds of animals that will be more productive.
   c. Selects animals to be used to provide energy in breeder reactors.

Exploring Careers—Instructor's Guide ©1990, JIST Works, Inc., Indianapolis, Indiana

FORESTER

A. Plan and take part in a science club activity at your school. Activities might include planting trees, pulling weeds, controlling insects, and other outdoor activities.

B. Volunteer to help with clearing brush, cleaning up a stream, or some other activity that helps our environment.

C. Try some outdoor hobbies such as hiking, fishing, camping, and birdwatching.

D. Make a map of your neighborhood or a small park in your area. On the map, show all the trees in the area, their type, and their approximate size. See if you can devise a code for doing this. P 60/20, for example, might indicate a stand of 60 pin trees, each about 20 feet tall. Using the map you have prepared, see if you can determine what areas could perhaps be thinned and what areas might benefit from a tree planting program.

E. Get a summer job working on a farm, or find other outdoor summer employment, such as being a camp counselor. Mowing lawns, working in a nursery, and gardening are other good possibilities.

F. Locate the nearest county, state or Federal forest in your area. Invite the forester in charge to speak to your class about his or her job. Prepare questions in advance.

G. If there is a logging or lumber company in your area, call the public relations department and ask if a speaker would be willing to visit your class and explain the company's operations.

H. Use forestry as a topic for class assignments. Do a report on the lumber industry for a social studies class. Prepare a report on different kinds of wood, their characteristics and uses, for a science class.

I. Help teach youngsters about the outdoors. You might lead nature walks and help youngsters identify trees, plants, flowers, insects, birds, and other wildlife. Volunteer your services to a day camp, community center, school, or church.

J. Join a farming organization for young people such as the Future Farmers of America or the 4-H Club. Members of these organizations gain practical experience in agriculture and take part in fairs, agricultural contests, horse shows, and many other activities.

K. If you are a Boy Scout, try for merit badges in Agriculture, Bird Study, Botany, Camping, Environmental Science, Fish and Wildlife Management, Forestry, Gardening, Insect Life, nature, Plant Science, Pulp and Paper, Soil and Water Conservation, Surveying, Wildlife Management, and Wilderness Survival.

L. If you are a Girl Scout, see if your local troop has the From Dreams to Reality program of career exploration. Troops may also offer opportunities to try out careers through internships, service aide and community action projects, and proficiency badges in a number of areas including Animal Kingdom, Campcraft, Conservation, Family Camper, Food Raiser, Games Leader, Hiker, Outdoor Safety, and Plant Kingdom.

M. Join an Outdoor, Conservation/Ecology, Agriculture, Hunting, Fishing, or Natural Science Explorer Post if there is one in your area. Exploring is open to young men and women aged 14 through 20. To find out about Explorer posts in your area, call "Boy Scouts of America" listed in your phone book, and ask for the "Exploring Division."

N. For more information about careers in forestry, write to the Society of American Foresters, 5400 Grosvenor Lane, Washington, D.C. 20814; American Forest Institute, 1619 Massachusetts Avenue, N.W., Washington, D.C. 20036; U.S. Department of Agriculture, Forest Service, Washington, D.C. 20013.

FORESTER

ACTIVITY 47

Name _____
Class _____

FORESTER
Related Occupations

Foresters are not the only workers concerned with managing and protecting our natural resources. Using the descriptions below, unscramble the letters to find the names of some of these other workers. Write your answers in the space provided.

1. **STROFERY IDAE.** I help foresters care for and manage forest lands and their resources. I may estimate the amount of wood a stand of timber contains, check trees for disease, or assist foresters in other ways.

   _____

2. **REMARF.** I plan, till, plant, fertilize, cultivate, and harvest crops. In many ways, my work is similar to a forester's.

   _____

3. **FIELDWIL LIOBISTGO.** I manage different types of land so that they will support animals such as deer, quail, and other wildlife. I may also do research on these animals and how they interact with their environment.

   _____

4. **GENAR NAGAMER.** I manage, improve, and protect our rangelands to make the best use of them without harming them. I may restore or improve rangelands through techniques such as controlled burning, reseeding, and controlling weeds.

   _____

5. **LOIS SERVCONISTATION.** I give technical help to farmers and other people concerned with the conservation of soil and water. If a farmer has a problem with soil erosion caused by water runoff, for example, I may recommend that the land be terraced.

   _____

Exploring Careers—Instructor's Guide ©1990, JIST Works, Inc., Indianapolis, Indiana

EXPLORING CAREERS ANSWER KEY

Activity 1   **ASSEMBLER**
1. Sewing machine operator, 2. Spray painter, 3. Machine cutter, 4. Automatic print developer, 5. Machine packager, 6. Yarn winder, 7. Ampoule filler, 8. Cannery worker, 9. Knitting machine operator.

Activity 2   **MACHINIST** - related occupations
1. b, 2. c, 3. g, 4. h, 5. e, 6. d, 7. a, 8. f.

Activity 3   **MACHINIST** - math
1. Three 2-meter bars with 90 centimeters of steel left over, 2. 35 teeth, 3. yes

Activity 4   **PHOTOCOMPOSITOR**
1. Printing press operator, 2. Proofreader, 3. Photoengraver, 4. Bookbinder, 5. Printing sales representative, 6. Layout artist, 7. Production manager.

Activity 5   **BANK OFFICER**
1. a, 2. c, 3. b, 4. c, 5. b, 6. c, 7. b, 8. a.

Activity 6   **PLANNER**
1. d, 2. b, 3. c, 4. f, 5. g, 6. a, 7. e.

Activity 7   **COMPUTER PROGRAMMER/SYSTEMS ANALYST**
1. Mathematician, 2. Actuary, 3. Operations research analyst, 4. Mathematical technician, 5. Statistician, 6. Financial analyst.

Activity 8   **CHEF** - related activities

		C	A	F	E	T	E	R	I	A	C	O	O	K		
B	R	O	I	L	E	R	C	O	O	K						
A	A		E				A								D	
N		K	X			P	A	S	T	R	Y	C	H	E	F	
Q			E				T							R	E	S
U			C	R			C		K				R	Y		S
E			U		F	O	O				E		C	H	E	
T			T		E	O			K				O		R	
C			I		H	C	K			A			R	O		T
H			V	C	P				M			T	K		C	
E			E	E	U			D			O				O	
F			C	O		A			R						O	
		U	H	S		L		D							K	
	A	V	E	G	E	T	A	B	L	E	C	O	O	K		
S			F		S		R									
				S	P	E	C	I	A	L	T	Y	C	O	O	K
				K	O	O	C	E	U	C	E	B	R	A	B	
				S	O	U	S	C	H	E	F					
				K					C	A	T	E	R	E	R	

EXPLORING CAREERS ANSWER KEY

Activity 9   **CHEF** - math
Cookbook problem.
a. 20 lbs. meat, 20 lbs. potatoes, 50 carrots, 10 onions, 10 teaspoons salt, 10 cups vegetables; b. To feed 60 people, you must spend $43.90; c. With a 25 percent discount, the cost will be $32.93.
Metric measurements.
1 teaspoon butter = approximately 2.5 grams,
1 tablespoon salt = approximately 7.5 grams,
1 cup flour = approximately 120 grams.

Activity 10   **BUILDING SERVICE WORKER**
1. Housekeeper, 2. Gardener, 3. Private household worker, 4. Boiler tender, 5. Painter, 6. Pest controller, 7. Maintenance electrician, 8. Trash collector, 9. Floor waxer, 10. Janitor, 11. Building superintendent, 12. Window cleaner.

Activity 11   **HOTEL CLERK**

T		C	U	S	T	O	M	E	R	C	O	M	P	L	A	I	N	T	C	L	E	R	K		
O														I											
U														C											
R	E	C	E	P	T	I	O	N	I	S	T			K					R			I			
G	K												E					E			N				
U	R							T	N	E	G	A	L	E	V	A	R	T			H			F	
I	E												A						S			O		
D	L												G						U			R		
E	C												E						R			M		
	N												N						E			A		
	O								T	N	A	D	N	E	T	T	A	H	G	I	L	F	T			T	
S	I	G	H	T	S	E	E	I	N	G	G	U	I	D	E				A			I		
	T																		E			O		
P	A	S	S	E	N	G	E	R	T	R	A	I	N	C	O	N	D	U	C	T	O	R	H			M	
E	V	I	T	A	T	N	E	S	E	R	P	E	R	E	C	I	V	R	E	S	R	E	M	O	T	S	U	C
	R																						L		
	E																						E		
	S																						R		
	E																						K		
	R																								

Activity 12   **POLICE OFFICER**
1. Detective, 2. Police photographer, 3. FBI special agent, 4. Sheriff, 5. Probation officer, 6. State police trooper, 7. Police chief, 8. Community relations officer, 9. Police academy instructor, 10. Fingerprint specialist.

Activity 13   **LIBRARIAN**
1. Media specialist, 2. Bibliographer, 3. Classifier, 4. Acquisitions librarian, 5. Reference librarian, 6. Bookmobile librarian, 7. Medical librarian, 8. Chief librarian.

EXPLORING CAREERS ANSWER KEY

Activity 14   **SECONDARY SCHOOL TEACHER**
1. Industrial arts teacher, 2; 2. Cooking teacher, 11; 3. Library science teacher, 3; 4. Law professor, 7; 5. Modeling teacher, 8; 6. Flying instructor, 14; 7. Engineering teacher, 10; 8. Watchmaking teacher, 6; 9. Nursing teacher, 4; 10. Economics teacher, 12; 11. Home economics teacher, 13; 12. Art teacher, 9; 13. Forestry teacher, 1; 14. Shop math teacher, 5.

Activity 15   **SCHOOL COUNSELOR**
1. Teacher, 2. Social worker, 3. Rabbi, 4. Employment counselor, 5. Priest, 6. Rehabilitation counselor, 7. Minister, 8. College career planning and placement counselor.

Activity 16   **SECURITIES SALES WORKER** - related occupations
1. Insurance agent and broker, 2. Real estate agent and broker, 3. Automobile sales worker, 4. Yacht broker, 5. Security analyst, 6. Order clerk, 7. Margin trader, 8. Bond trader.

Activity 17   **SECURITIES SALES WORKER** - math
AC&C, American Railroad Co., and D.C. Electric Co. would provide a higher yield than the savings account.

Activity 18   **AUTOMOBILE PARTS COUNTER WORKER**
1. Manufacturer's representative, 2. Automobile sales worker, 3. Automobile service adviser, 4. Automobile mechanic, 5. Gasoline service station attendant.

Activity 19   **GASOLINE SERVICE STATION ATTENDANT**
1. Retail trade sales clerk, 2. Dining room attendant, 3. Dishwasher, 4. Animal caretaker, 5. Usher, 6. Foundation worker, 7. Library clerk, 8. Vehicle washer, 9. Health trainee, 10. Newspaper vendor, 11. Cashier, 12. Amusement attendant, 13. Messenger, 14. Stock handler.

Activity 20   **BRICKLAYER** - related occupations
1. Cement mason, 2. Tilesetter, 3. Terrazzo worker, 4. Stonemason, 5. Hod carrier or mason tender, 6. Marble setter.

Activity 21   **BRICKLAYER** - math
1. 212 inches or 17-2/3 feet, 2. 12 hours or 1-1/2 days, 3. 3,080 bricks, 4. 8.75 cubic yards.

Activity 22   **CARPENTER** - related occupations
1. d, 2. e, 3. g, 4. f, 5. a, 6. c, 7. b.

Activity 23   **CARPENTER** - math
1. 10 turns, 2, 48 boards, 3. 6-3/8 inches, 4. 35 hours = 4- 3/8 8-hour days.

Activity 24   **PLUMBER** - related occupations
1. Air-conditioning, refrigeration, and heating mechanic, 2. Welder, 3. Sheet-metal worker, 4. Water treatment plant operator, 5. Sprinkler fitter.

Activity 25   **PLUMBER** - math
1. 25.5 pounds per square inch, 2. 13.5 feet, 3. 60 pounds, 4. 96-2/3 feet, 5. 9 gallons weighing 75 pounds.

EXPLORING CAREERS ANSWER KEY

Activity 26   **AIR TRAFFIC CONTROLLER**
1. Airplane mechanic, 2. Airplane maintenance crew, 3. Baggage handler, 4. Co-pilot, 5. Dispatcher, 6. Electronics technician, 7. En route traffic controller, 8. Flight attendant, 9. Flight engineer, 10. Passenger agent, 11. Pilot, 12. Reservation agent, 13. Ticket agent.

Activity 27   **RAILROAD PASSENGER CONDUCTOR**

(Word search grid containing: ELECTRICAL WORKERS, SREKAMRELIOB (BOILERMAKERS reversed), BRAKE OPERATOR, STSINIHCAM (MACHINISTS reversed), ENGINEER, TELEGRAPHERS, STATION AGENTS, SRENIATNIAM LANGIS (SIGNAL MAINTAINERS reversed), TOWER WORKERS, TRACK WORKERS, SIGNAL INSTALLERS, SHEET METAL WORKERS, and vertical words BLACKSMITHS, DISPATCHERS.)

Activity 28   **BUS DRIVER**
1. d, 2. f, 3. a, 4. h, 5. e, 6. b, 7. g, 8. c.

Activity 29   **BIOCHEMIST**
1. a, 2. c, 3. a, 4. b, 5. b, 6. c, 7. a.

Activity 30   **ELECTRICAL ENGINEER**
1. Marine, 2. Mechanical, 3. Nuclear, 4. Aeronautical, 5. Ceramic, 6. Chemical, 7. Civil, 8. Transportation, 9. Automotive, 10. Optical.

Activity 31   **AUTO MECHANIC**
1. Aircraft mechanic, 2. bicycle repairer, 3. Boat engine mechanic, 4. Bus mechanic, 5. Diesel mechanic, 6. Farm equipment mechanic, 7. Motorcycle mechanic, 8. Small engine mechanic, 9. Truck mechanic.

Activity 32   **COMPUTER SERVICE TECHNICIAN**
1. Appliance repairer, 2. Automotive electrician, 3. Business machine mechanic, 4. Electronic organ technician, 5. Instrument repairer, 6. Radio repairer, 7. Radar repairer, 8. TV service technician.

Activity 33   **JEWELER**
1. Automobile body repairer, 2. Machinist, 3. Modelmaker, 4. Tool maker, 5. Silversmith, 6. Goldsmith, 7. Watch repairer.

Activity 34   **REGISTERED NURSE**
1. b, 2. c, 3. b, 4. a, 5. a, 6. b, 7. c, 8. b, 9. a, 10. c.

EXPLORING CAREERS ANSWER KEY

Activity 35 **MEDICAL TECHNOLOGIST**
1. b, 2. c, 3. a, 4. b, 5. a, 6. c, 7. b, 8. a, 9. c, 10. b.

Activity 36 **PHYSICAL THERAPIST**
1. Art therapist, 2. Prosthetist, 3. Occupational therapist, 4. Chiropractor, 5. Speech pathologist or audiologist, 6. Music therapist, 7. Osteopathic physician, 8. Physical therapist assistant or aide, 9. Orthopedic surgeon, 10. Recreational therapist, 11. Dance therapist, 12. Occupational therapy assistant, 13. Respiratory therapy worker.

Activity 37 **MUSEUM CURATOR**
1. Biographer, 2. Archivist, 3. Museum technician, 4. Restorer, lace and textiles, 5. Conservation technician, 6. Genealogist, 7. Archaeologist, 8. Art conservator, 9. Armorer technician, 10. Paintings restorer, 11. Supervisor, historic sites, 12. Fine arts packer.

Activity 38 **MINISTER**
1. Rabbi, 2. Chaplain, 3. Social worker, 4. Priest, 5. Missionary, 6. School counselor, 7. Christian Science practitioner, 8. Psychologist.

Activity 39 **SOCIAL WORKER**
1. Parole officer, 2. Recreation leader, 3. Caseworker, 4. Minister, 5. Probation officer, 6. School counselor, 7. Community organization worker, 8. Social welfare administrator.

Activity 40 **ARCHITECT** - related occupations
1. b, 2. g, 3. d, 4. f, 5. h, 6. a, 7. c, 8. e.

Activity 41 **ARCHITECT** - math
1. 2000 sq. ft.; 2. 4 ft. x 5 ft. x 10 ft., 5 ft. x 5 ft. x 8 ft., 10ft. x 10 ft. x 2 ft.; 3. $15,000.

Activity 42 **NEWSPAPER REPORTER**

EXPLORING CAREERS ANSWER KEY

Activity 43   **MUSICIAN**

```
I   B       O R C H E S T R A T O R       I
  N A I R A R B I L C I S U M             N
    S       C H U R C H M U S I C I A N   S
I N S T R U M E N T A L I S T   M     M   T
  A       R                 U     U   R
  I     M U S I C O L O G I S T   S   U
  C       M   V O C A L I S T   I O   M
  I   R     E       C   R   C   P     E
  S   O   P I A N I S T   E   C   E   N
  U   T       T E   S   R     R N     T
  M   C       A S O   I     A A       C
  K   U Y     C   P A T     R S I     R
  L   D E   H   M   I L     R I C     A
  O   N K   E   O   C   E   A N I     F
  F   O C R   C         S   N G S     T
  R E C O R D P R O D U C E R P   G E U   S
        J                     E E R M     P
M U S I C T H E R A P I S T       R K     E
        S T U D I O M U S I C I A N S C   R
  M U S I C T H E A T E R D I R E C T O R S
        D                         R N O
        R O T C E R I D S U R O H C       N
```

Activity 44   **FARMER** - related occupations
1. Farm manager, 2. Farm equipment mechanic, 3. Farm laborer, 4. Agricultural pilot, 5. Agricultural products broker, 6. Veterinarian.

Activity 45   **FARMER** - math
1. 24,000 bushels; 2. a. $2.50 per bushel, b. $3.50 per bushel; 3. $2,240, 4. $1.20 profit for each bushel fed.

Activity 46   **COOPERATIVE EXTENSION SERVICE WORKER**
1. a, 2. b, 3. a, 4. c, 5. b.

Activity 47   **FORESTER**
1. Forestry aide, 2. Farmer, 3. Wildlife biologist, 4. Range manager, 5. Soil conservationist.

Exploring Careers—Instructor's Guide   ©1990, JIST WORKS, Inc., Indianapolis, Indiana